D1477146

JIM CLARK TO JACKIE STEWART

Motor racing in the 1960s

BRYAN APPS

HALSGROVE

First published in Great Britain in 2012

Copyright © Bryan Apps 2012

British Library Cataloguing-in-Publication Data
A CIP record for this title is available from the British Library

ISBN 978 0 85704 189 0

HALSGROVE
Halsgrove House,
Ryelands Business Park,
Bagley Road, Wellington, Somerset TA21 9PZ
Tel: 01823 653777   Fax: 01823 216796
email: sales@halsgrove.com

Part of the Halsgrove group of companies.
Information on all Halsgrove titles is available at: www.halsgrove.com

Printed in China by Everbest Printing Co Ltd

CONTENTS

BIBLIOGRAPHY

Motor Sport; *Autosport*; *Grand Prix* by Trevor R Griffiths; Grand Prix! by Mike Lang; Stirling Moss with Doug Nye; *Stirling Moss – the Champion Without a Crown* by Pierre Menard and Jacques Vassel; *All My Races* by Stirling Moss and Alan Henry; *The Concise Encyclopaedia of Formula One* by David Tremayne and Mark Hughes; *With Flying Colours* by L.J.K. Setright, Derek Forsyth and Robert Newman; *Formula One Unseen Archives* by Tim Hill; *Ferrari* by Hans Tanner with Doug Nye; *Ferrari – the Grand Prix Cars* by Alan Henry; *British Grand Prix* by Maurice Hamilton; *B.R.M.* by Raymond Mays and Peter Roberts; *A History of the World's Racing Cars* by Richard Hough and Michael Frostick; *Track Pass* by Geoff Goddard with Doug Nye; *Formula 1* by Rainer W Schlegelmilch and Hartmut Lehbrink; *British Cars at Le Mans* by Dominique Pascal; *Real Racers* by Stuart Codling; *Murray Walker's Formula One Heroes* by Murray Walker and Simon Taylor; *101 Brockbank Cartoons* with a foreword by Quentin Blake, *Scarlet Passion* by Anthony Pritchard.

Thanks are due to Colin Simmons and Grant Wells for their help in the compilation of this book.

A Word from Murray Walker

"For many it is a moot point whether Jim Clark or Jackie Stewart is the greatest driver of them all. They are both certainly right up there and Bryan Apps couldn't have chosen a more exciting and interesting era of motor sport for his latest book. Bryan's skill at capturing the essence of his subject is truly impressive and with such a fascinating time to record in his inimitable way the result is highly commendable."

Murray Walker
2012

Russell Brockbank cartoon
(reproduced with the kind permission
of the Brockbank Partnership).

INTRODUCTION

It has been said that if you can remember anything about the sixties you weren't really there, but "Jim Clark to Jackie Stewart" challenges that assertion on behalf of all those who like me were high on motor racing rather than drugs. It is also said that a single picture is worth more than a thousand words and for this reason I have illustrated many of my accounts of motor races in the 1960s, bringing colour to images which are usually seen in black and white. Every Formula 1 World Championship event is included and, for good measure, the Monte Carlo Rally, the 24 Hours of Le Mans, and the Targa Florio, raced over the mountainous Sicilian roads. In addition to Jim Clark and Jackie Stewart, the book also features the achievements of Stirling Moss, Jack Brabham, Graham Hill, John

Jochen Rindt in a 3 litre V12 Cooper-Maserati

Surtees and all the other famous drivers of the period. The cars of the 60s are given due prominence but it is always remembered that it was the drivers who brought them to life with their incredible skill, courage and competitive spirit.

The 1960s was an important decade for the development of the mid engined Formula 1 racing car, because it was in those years that it became broadly established in its settled form, with a monocoque body for lightness, strength and rigidity; "doughnut" tyres and aerofoils to glue it to the ground; anti roll bars to provide its driver with greater safety; a reclining driving position to reduce its height and, of course, sponsorship which would eventually lead, via Bernie Ecclestone, to unbridled wealth. Safety became a major issue in the 1960s, thanks in large measure to the efforts of Jackie Stewart. Many will remember how, with great moral courage, he led the Formula One Drivers' Association in 1969 to boycott the Belgian Grand Prix when the organisers had refused to introduce Armco barriers. More remained to be done both to the circuits and to the cars in the cause of safety and there were still too many tragic deaths which, with the gift of hindsight, can be seen to have been largely avoidable. The 1960s was also the decade of those whom Enzo Ferrari derisively called "the garagistes," when first Coventry-Climax and then Ford Cosworth enabled the likes of John Cooper and Colin Chapman to produce World Championship racing cars in workshops no bigger than garages, causing the B.R.Ms to be called the "British Ferraris.".

The first year of the 60s was also the last year of the 2.5 litre Formula which had given us such iconic cars as the 250F Maserati and the W196 Mercedes Benz. The new 1.5 litre Formula was dismissed by the editor of "Classic Driver" with his accusation that the "piddling 1.5 litre engines made the cars of the era toys." Yet it gave birth to some memorable cars including the Tipo 156 Ferrari, the P57 B.R.M. and the trend setting Lotus 25. If 1961 was effectively handed to the Italian Ferraris, the British teams soon caught up and some close and exciting races ensued. !966 brought power back to the World Championship Series, and the 3 litre Formula was responsible for the V12 Honda, the Cooper-Maserati, and the DFV Ford Cosworth engine which powered, amongst others, the Lotus 49 and Ken Tyrrell's Matra. Of course there's more to motor racing than engine capacity, and one of the greatest races of the 60s was at Monaco in 1961 when Stirling Moss successfully kept at bay the six cylinder Ferraris of Ritchie Ginther, Phil Hill and Wolfgang von Trips with Rob Walker's underpowered Lotus 18. Moss won the race over the narrow streets of Monaco at just 70.704 mph, after Alf Francis had welded a cracked chassis tube on the starting grid when the car was already laden with fuel! Sadly Stirling Moss' bid for a World Championship ended abruptly with his crash at Goodwood in 1962. It was on the day that Kath and I were married and Stirling told me 40 years later that, on the anniversary of the day which for very different reasons held memories for us all, he and Susie drank our toast. There's only one Stirling Moss, but other drivers have also thrilled the crowds, and none more so than two young "Flying Scotsmen."

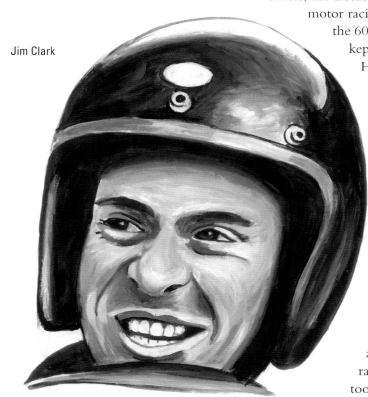
Jim Clark

Jim Clark and Jackie Stewart were the greatest of friends and the most immensely talented of racing drivers. Clark raced exclusively for Colin Chapman throughout his all too brief Formula 1 career and, in the course of six years, started in seventy-two World Championship Grands Prix and won twenty-five of them. He also convincingly won two World Championship titles in 1963 and 1965 in Chapman's innovative, fast but fragile Lotus cars. He also won the Indianapolis 500 Mile Race in 1965 in the Lotus 29, and he was renowned for taking a Lotus Cortina around Silverstone at incredible speed on three wheels. No one can say how much more Clark would have achieved had it not been for his fatal crash in a Formula 2 race at Hockenheim in 1968 when his car inexplicably crashed at top speed into the trees that lined the circuit.

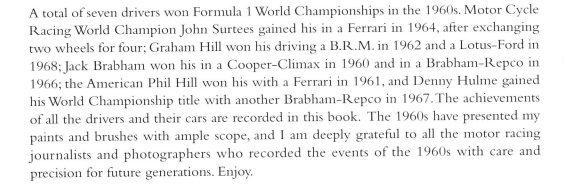

Jackie Stewart's introduction to Formula 1 was to drive Jim Clark's Lotus in the non Championship Rand Grand Prix in South Africa in 1964, but his entry into the Formula 1 World Championship Series was with B.R.M. in 1965. He won his first World Championship race at Monza that year, but his first World Championship title came in 1969 when he was driving Ken Tyrrell's Matra-Ford. He was to win two more World Championships in 1971 and 1973 driving Tyrrell-Fords. Stewart won a record breaking total of twenty-seven World Championship Grands Prix from ninety-nine starts, and he too would have added to his tally had he not chosen to retire when he did. Both Clark and Stewart had exceptional skills which were natural and instinctive, and which set them apart from others. In the course of many hours spent with Ken Tyrrell in the Tyrrell Pits and Motor Home at Silverstone I discovered that the highest accolade he would bestow upon any young driver was that he might one day develop into another Jackie Stewart.

Jackie Stewart

A total of seven drivers won Formula 1 World Championships in the 1960s. Motor Cycle Racing World Champion John Surtees gained his in a Ferrari in 1964, after exchanging two wheels for four; Graham Hill won his driving a B.R.M. in 1962 and a Lotus-Ford in 1968; Jack Brabham won his in a Cooper-Climax in 1960 and in a Brabham-Repco in 1966; the American Phil Hill won his with a Ferrari in 1961, and Denny Hulme gained his World Championship title with another Brabham-Repco in 1967. The achievements of all the drivers and their cars are recorded in this book. The 1960s have presented my paints and brushes with ample scope, and I am deeply grateful to all the motor racing journalists and photographers who recorded the events of the 1960s with care and precision for future generations. Enjoy.

1960
The end of an era

Practice times before the Argentina Grand Prix confirmed that the days of the front engined Formula 1 car were numbered. Stirling Moss was fastest in Rob Walker's Cooper-Climax and Innes Ireland was alongside him in the new rear engined Lotus 18 with its light aluminium body and fuel tanks. The front engined Dino 246 Ferraris of Wolfgang von Trips, Phil Hill and Cliff Allison could only manage 5th 6th and 7th on the starting grid. The Ferraris were beginning to be regarded as dinosaurs by irreverent enthusiasts as Graham Hill and Joakim Bonnier, in 3rd and 4th places, were also sitting in front of the engines of their P48 B.R.Ms. After the Dutch Grand Prix B.R.M. sent Peter Berthon to Harry Weslake Research in Sussex and put Tony Rudd in charge of the development of the new V8 engine in Bourne. Enzo Ferrari, who had adopted independent suspension on all four wheels of his 1960 cars, signalled a clear intention to follow the current trend with his rear engined Formula 2 car. The Dino 246 when it appeared at Monaco was driven by Richie Ginther as Tony Brooks had already left Ferrari to drive a Yeoman Credit Cooper. With only one year left for the 2.5 litre Formula to run its course a brave attempt to inject more life into it was made by Lance Reventlow from the United States with his front engined Scarabs. These cars were equipped with dual overhead cam four cylinder engines with desmodromic valves, fuel injection, Girling disc brakes, independent suspension on all four wheels and with the support of Reventlow's wealthy mother. Sadly, the Scarabs failed to make an impact, as also did the Grand Prix DBR5 Aston Martins which, though lighter than the DBR4s, were still too heavy and underpowered. What weighed most heavily in the minds of many was the knowledge that in twelve months time Formula 1 cars were going to be smaller, less powerful, presumably slower, and less impressive, but 1960 remained to be enjoyed. Jim Clark was to drive in his first Grand Prix at Zandvoort in 1960 and Jackie Stewart, whose brother Jimmy drove for Ecurie Ecosse and Aston Martin, would decline an invitation to test Barry Filer's Porsche 90 at Oulton Park rather than distress his mother.

Jack Brabham

THE WORLD CHAMPIONSHIP SERIES

Argentine Grand Prix February 7

Graham Hill had joined Joakim Bonnier at B.R.M. for 1960, commencing what would grow into his long and fruitful relationship with the team at Bourne. Innes Ireland was entrusted with the new rear engined Lotus 18 while Alan Stacy was given a 1959 Lotus 16. Stirling Moss and Maurice Trintignant drove Rob Walker's Cooper-Climax cars and Jack Brabham once again led the works Cooper team. Tony Brooks had a Yeoman Credit Cooper and the drivers of the Dino 246 Ferraris were Wolfgang von Trips, Phil Hill, Cliff Allison and Froilan Gonzales. Carlos Menditguy drove a 4 cylinder Cooper-Maserati. Following practice, the front row of the grid consisted of Stirling Moss, Innes Ireland, Graham Hill and Joakim Bonnier. Ireland was encouraged by the performance of the new Lotus and Graham Hill was impressed by his front engined P25 B.R.M, the P48s not yet being ready.

Ireland led for the first two laps of the race but then dropped back after a spin. Then it was the B.R.Ms of Bonnier and Graham Hill who led the way and they were followed by Brabham, Moss, Ireland and Phil Hill in the first of the Ferraris. Moss overtook Brabham, who was in some difficulty, and then Graham Hill, thus splitting the two B.R.Ms. Then on lap 14 Moss also passed Bonnier who was at this stage being followed by Ireland, Brabham and Graham Hill. It was an extremely hot afternoon and Antonio Creus (Maserati), Ettore Chimera (Maserati) and Alan Stacey were all forced to retire through heat exhaustion. Graham Hill retired on lap 38, with his car overheating, and Moss came in on lap 41 with gearbox trouble after successfully denying Bonnier the lead. Next Bonnier had to surrender an apparently secure lead as his B.R.M. was running too hot. Ireland dropped back with a misfire and Bruce McLaren's works Cooper-Climax, which had started in only 13th place, continued to make steady progress through the field to cross the finishing line first, and ahead of Allison's Ferrari. Trintignant's Cooper-Climax, with Moss now at the wheel, had stormed through, its driver offering a master class to delighted the spectators, to finish third.

Bruce McLaren won the race at 82.771 mph while Moss established the fastest lap of the race at 88.482 mph.

Monaco Grand Prix: May 29

Among the entries at Monaco were two new and beautifully engineered Scarabs from the United States, finished in blue and white. They were equipped with Chevrolet Corvette gearboxes and driven by Chuck Daigh and Lance Reventlow himself, both sitting very low in their cars alongside their propeller shafts. A Ferrari engined Cooper-Castellotti was to be driven by Giorgio Scarlatti but all three of these newcomers failed to qualify for the race. B.R.M. arrived with three of their new rear engined P48 cars but it was Stirling Moss who was in pole position in Rob Walker's brand new Climax engined Lotus 18. He had Jack Brabham and Tony Brooks alongside him in Cooper-Climax cars, both Brooks and Chris Bristow being in Yeoman Credit cars. Of the B.R.Ms, Joakim Bonnier's was 5th, Graham Hill's 6th, and Dan Gurney's 14th. Wolfgang von Trips' Ferrari was 8th, and the Ferrari's of Richie Ginther and Phil Hill 9th and 10th. John Surtees, sitting in a car instead of a motorcycle, was back in 15th in a works Lotus 18. Chris Allison was excluded by the injuries he sustained when his Ferrari crashed in practice for the race. Works Lotus-Climaxes were also driven by Innes Ireland and Alan Stacey and, for good measure, there were three Centro-Sud 4 cylinder Cooper-Maseratis driven by Maurice Trintignant, Masten Gregory and Ian Burgess.

At the start of the race Bonnier came through from the second row to lead from Brabham and Moss. Then Moss, having passed Brabham, eventually overtook the B.R.M. on lap 17, Bonnier waving him past with fading brakes. The positions remained unchanged until lap 34 when Brabham overtook Moss only to spin out of contention with gearbox

Stirling Moss winning the
Monaco Grand Prix in Rob
Walker's new Lotus 18.

Stirling Moss winning the Monaco Grand Prix in Rob Walker's new Lotus 18.

trouble. Moss now led Bonnier by a useful margin and he was followed by Bruce McLaren (Cooper-Climax), Graham Hill (B.R.M.) and Phil Hill (Ferrari). Moss had to pit on lap 60 to have a plug lead secured but soon overtook Bonnier once more. McLaren and Graham Hill spun on the slippery surface and Bonnier had to give up at last with a rear suspension failure. Only four cars were running at the end and they crossed the line in the order of Moss, McLaren, Phil Hill and Tony Brooks. **Stirling Moss' winning average speed was 67.480 mph** and the fastest lap was established by McLaren at 73.131 mph.

Dutch Grand Prix: June 6

The 1960 version of the DBR4 Aston Martin which arrived at Zandvoort for Roy Salvadori to drive was lighter but less manageable than the 1959 car. It was also tried briefly by Stirling Moss during practice but Salvadori, excellent driver though he undoubtedly was, failed to lap fast enough to make it to the starting grid. The race was most notable for the fact that it was Jim Clark's first Formula 1 World Championship race.

Graham Hill in the P 48 B.R.M. at Zandvoort being followed by Jim Clark who was competing in his first World Championship race.

He managed a modest 11th place in the fifth row of the grid in his works Lotus 18. At the front was Stirling Moss (Lotus-Climax), Jack Brabham (Cooper-Climax) and Innes Ireland (Lotus-Climax). There were ten Coventry-Climax engine cars in the line up which also included the Maserati engined Cooper of Maurice Trintignant. The B.R.Ms of Joakim Bonnier, Graham Hill and Dan Gurney were 4th, 5th and 6th and the Ferraris of Richie Ginther, Phil Hill and Wolfgang von Trips only 12th 13th and 15th.

It was Brabham who led away at the start closely followed by Moss, Ireland (Lotus-Climax), Alan Stacey (Lotus-Climax) and Bruce McLaren (Cooper-Climax). Gurney (B.R.M.) moved up to fifth place after McLaren dropped out with mechanical trouble on lap 9. Three laps later Gurney crashed out at 140 mph when his brake pipe broke and, while he himself wasn't seriously injured, a spectator was killed. Moss was running in close company with Brabham when he had a puncture as the result of some debris thrown up by Brabham's Cooper and so was delayed at his pit. Behind Brabham, Ireland and Alan Stacey, Graham Hill was contending with Clark, enjoying his first Formula 1 Grand Prix until his Lotus retired with mechanical problems. Stacey was forced to retire with transmission problems and **Jack Brabham emerged as the clear winner at 96.268 mph.** He was followed by Ireland, Graham Hill and Moss, the last named having set the fastest lap of the race at 99.994 mph.

Belgian Grand Prix: June 19

Both Stirling Moss and Michael Taylor crashed their Lotus 18s during practice at Spa, Moss injuring his back, nose and leg while Taylor sustained a broken collar bone. It might have been regarded as a bad omen for the race. At the end of practice the order at the front of the grid was Jack Brabham (Cooper), Tony Brooks (Cooper and Phil Hill (Ferrari).

Chuck Daigh's Scarab during
its brief appearance in the
Belgian Grand Prix

Graham Hill's B.R.M. before its
retirement from the tragic
Belgian Grand Prix.

Olivier Gendebien (Cooper-Climax) and Graham Hill (B.R.M.) occupied the second row while Jim Clark (Lotus-Climax) was on the 4th row in 9th place.

On the first lap Brabham and Olivier Gendebien (Yeoman Credit Cooper-Climax) were at the head of a closely packed field while, one lap later, Lance Reventlow's Scarab disappointingly pulled out with a blown engine. Then Phil Hill moved up to second place behind Brabham, the two putting some distance between themselves and the following cars. Joakim Bonnier (B.R.M.) dropped back from third place and retired on lap 15 and the order became Brabham, Phil Hill and Gendebien. Then tragically on lap 19 Chris Bristow, who had been dicing with Willy Mairesse, swerved off the circuit at speed and into a bank. He was thrown out and killed instantly. Five laps later Alan Stacey also in Cooper-Climax, lost control of his car on the Malmedy curve when he was hit by a bird. He too was killed after being thrown from his car. **The race was won by Brabham at 133.625 mph** from the Coopers of Bruce McLaren and Gendebien. Graham Hill retired on lap 36 with engine trouble. The fastest lap of this sad race was recorded jointly by Brabham, Phil Hill and Innes Ireland (Lotus) at 136.010 mph. Jim Clark had been cruelly confronted with the extreme dangers of Grand Prix racing early in his career. He finished in 5th place, two laps behind the winner.

French Grand Prix: July 3

Tony Brooks arrived at Rheims with a new front engined Vanwall which was lower than the earlier car, had a new 5 speed gearbox and a short rounded tail. He could achieve no better than 14th place with it in practice. At the front were Jack Brabham (Cooper-Climax) Phil Hill (Ferrari) and Graham Hill (B.R.M.). Of the works Lotus drivers Innes Ireland was 4th and Jim Clark 12th. Stirling Moss was an absentee as he was recovering from his injuries at Spa.

Graham Hill was left at the start sorting out his gears and he was promptly shunted by Maurice Trintignant's Cooper-Maserati, the two in consequence being eliminated from the race. Brabham predictably led the race, but only just, from the Ferraris of Phil Hill and Wolfgang von Trips. The first two swopped the lead more than once while the Vanwall retired without distinction on lap 8, Brooks having briefly pitted on lap 4 to have the source of a vibration inspected. For the entire first half of the race the spectators were treated to a high speed chase in which the Cooper and the two Ferraris swopped the lead with none of them able to gain a clear advantage. Eventually Brabham managed to achieve a cushion of 5 seconds after establishing a new lap record at 135.057 mph. Soon after this the Ferraris of Phil Hill and von Trips were both forced to pull out of the race with transmission problems, although Hill was credited with having finished in 12th place. Olivier Gendebien (Cooper-Climax) and Bruce McLaren (Cooper-Climax) finished second and third to **Brabham who won the race at an average speed of 131.801 mph**. Jim Clark and Innes Ireland finished in 5th and 7th places.

British Grand Prix: July 16

With the Scarabs back in America Lance Reventlow drove a works Cooper of 1959 vintage while Jack Brabham and Bruce McLaren had 1960 cars. Tony Brooks, Olivier Gendebien and Henry Taylor drove Yeoman Credit Coopers while Roy Salvadori and Maurice Trintignant had the two DBR4 Aston Martins, now fitted with Weber carburetters.

Once more Jack Brabham's Cooper-Climax was fastest in practice and the B.R.Ms of Graham Hill and Joakim Bonnier were on either side of Bruce McLaren's Cooper-Climax, the three completing the front row of four cars. Jim Clark and John Surtees were both on the third row of the grid in 8th and 11th places, and the Aston Martins were back in 13th and 21st places.

Opposite, top: Jim Clark's Lotus 18 leading Henry Taylor's Yeoman Credit Cooper-Climax and John Surtees' Lotus-Climax during the British Grand Prix.

Opposite, bottom: Graham Hill's B.R.M. flat out during his epic drive in the 1960 British Grand Prix.

The Starting Grid

J. Bonnier	B. McLaren	Graham Hill	J. Brabham
B.R.M	Cooper-Climax	B.R.M	Cooper-Climax
1 min 36.2 secs	1 min 36.0 secs	1 min 35.6 secs	1 min 34.6 secs

W. von Trips	D. Gurney	I. Ireland
Ferrari	B.R.M	Lotus-Climax
I min 37.0 secs	1 min 36.6 secs	1 min 36.2 secs

J. Surtees	Phil Hil	T. Brooks	J. Clark
Lotus-Climax	Ferrari	Cooper-Climax	Lotus-Climax
1 min 38.6 secs	1 min 37.8 secs	1 min 37.6 secs	1 min 37 secs

M. Gregory	R. Salvadori	O. Gendebien
Cooper-Maserati	Aston Martin	Cooper-Climax
1 min 39.8 secs	1 min 39.4 secs	1 min 39.2 secs

B. Naylor	G. Bianchi	H. Taylor	J. Fairman
Cooper-Maserati	Cooper-Climax	Cooper-Climax	Cooper-Climax
1 min 41.2 secs	1 min 40.2 secs	1 min 40.0 secs	1 min 39.8 secs

M. Trintignant	I. Burgess	C. Daigh
Aston Martin	Cooper-Maserati	Cooper-Climax
1 min 43.8 secs	1 min 42.6 secs	1 min 42.4 secs

G. Munaron	D. Piper	K. Greene
Cooper-Ferrari	Lotus-Climax	Cooper-Maserati
Failed to Practice	2 min 05.6 secs	1 min 45.8 secs

Jack Brabham the eventual winner of the British Grand Prix.

Stirling Moss, not yet fully recovered from his crash at Spa, was the official starter and he saw the pack stream past Graham Hill, Brooks and Taylor as all three had stalled on the line. Out in front Bruce McLaren led Brabham briefly and, as the race settled down, the order was Brabham followed by McLaren, Joakim Bonnier, and Ireland. Once he got started Graham Hill began a meteoric drive from last place but one. On lap 9 he passed the two Ferraris and he was in 7th place by lap 11. At 20 laps the order was Brabham (Cooper-Climax) Ireland (Cooper-Climax) Surtees (Lotus-Climax) Clark (Lotus-Climax) Bruce McLaren (Cooper-Climax) and Graham Hill (B.R.M.). On lap 30 Hill was in 3rd place with only the Coopers of Brabham and Ireland ahead of him. Then on lap 55 the B.R.M. swept into the lead, followed by Brabham, Surtees, Ireland, McLaren and Brooks. It seemed that a B.R.M. must win a British Grand Prix at last but Brabham was not to be left behind and continued to press Hill all the way round the circuit for lap after lap. Finally, on lap 72, five laps from the end of the race, Graham Hill, exhausted after his epic drive and suffering with failing brakes, spun at Copse Corner and his race was over. Brabham waved to him in sympathy as he passed Hill's stationary car, and Hill walked back to his pit. Having gained several places earlier in the race Jim Clark was put out of contention by broken rear suspension. **Brabham won the race from Surtees by 50 seconds at a speed of 108.69 mph.** It was a great second place for John Surtees, so newly arrived in the motor racing world, but the fastest lap was attributed to Graham Hill at 111.62 mph.

Results

1. Jack Brabham   Cooper-Climax   2 hr. 04 min 24.6 secs.
2. John Surtees   Lotus-Climax   2 hr. 05 min 14.2 secs
3. Innes Ireland   Lotus-Climax   2 hr 05 min 54.2 secs
4. Bruce McLaren Cooper-Climax   1 lap
5 Tony Brooks   Cooper-Climax
6. Wolfgang von Trips Ferrari   2 laps
7. Phil Hill   Ferrari
8. Henry Taylor Cooper-Climax   3 laps
9. Olivier Gendebien Cooper-Climax
10. Dan Gurney   B.R.M
11. Maurice Trintignant Aston Martin   5 laps
12. David Piper Lotus-Climax
13. Brian Naylor Cooper-Maserati
14. Masten Gregory Cooper-Maserati   6 laps
15. Gino Muneron Cooper-Ferrari   7 laps
16. Jim Clark Lotus-Climax

Retirements

Keith Greene Cooper-Maserati lap 13 overheating
Roy Salvadori Aston Martin lap 45 steering
Jack Fairman Cooper-Climax lap 45 fuel pump
Ian Burgess Cooper-Maserati lap 57 valves
Chuck Daigh Cooper-Climax lap 57 overheating
Joakim Bonnier B.R.M. lap 60 rear suspension
Lucien Bianchi Ccooper-Climax lap 61 engine
Graham Hill lap 72 spin.

Grand Prix of Portugal: August 14

Stirling Moss had recovered from his injuries in time to drive Rob Walker's rebuilt Lotus 18 in the Portuguese Grand Prix in Oporto on a true road circuit which even featured tram lines and cobbles! There were four B.R.Ms on hand and Cooper-Maseratis for Masten Gregory and Mario Cabral. Henry Taylor's Cooper-Climax overturned during

practice without serious injury to the driver but he was consequently unable to start the race. Dan Gurney, going well in his B.R.M, was second on the starting grid to John Surtees (Lotus-Climax), now already a front runner in Formula 1, with Jack Brabham's Cooper-Climax in third place. Stirling Moss occupied the second row with Graham Hill's B.R.M. Jim Clark (Lotus-Climax), who had bent his car after a slight excursion during practice while trying to avoid the tramlines, was 8th fastest, and the Ferraris of Wolfgang von Trips and Phil Hill 9th and 10th.

There was some creeping before the start which was initiated by Graham Hill, but it was Gurney who led into the first bend where he was promptly cut out and relegated to 2rd place by Brabham. The B.R.M. was ahead again before the lap was over while von Trips took to the straw bales. Moss and Surtees were not far behind the leading pair and, after the opening laps the order was Gurney, Surtees, Moss and Brabham while Bonnier (B.R.M.) who had been well up, dropped out with engine trouble on lap 7. Gurney went out on lap 25, also with engine trouble, after a fine drive and then it was Surtees' turn to lead from Phil Hill and Brabham. On lap 29 the Ferrari driver hit the wrong gear and so ended his race in the straw bales. Then Surtees, who was in trouble with fuel leaking into his cockpit and over his brake pedal, struck a kerb and consequently retired on lap 37 with a damaged radiator. **Brabham was handed his fifth win in a row at 109.267 mph,** followed by Bruce McLaren (Cooper-Climax), Clark, von Trips and Tony Brooks (Cooper-Climax). The fastest lap was established by Surtees at 112.309 mph.

Italian Grand Prix: September 4

The British works teams were conspicuous by their absence at Monza as they had all declined to use the banked circuit. This resulted in the three Ferraris of Phil Hill, Richie Ginther and Willy Mairesse filling the front row of the grid, Ginther's being a long chassis model. Wolfgang von Trips was 6th in a Formula 2 Ferrari. A brand new rear engined Formula 1 Ferrari was also brought along but it was not used. Giullo Cabianca (Cooper-Ferrari) and Giorgio Scarlatti (Cooper-Maserati) were 4th and 5th. There were a number of F2 Porsches further down the grid including two works cars for Hans Herrmann and Edgar Barth, and two Centro Sud Cooper-Maseratis for Giorgio Scarlatti and Alfonso Thiele.

Phil Hill gaining the last World Championship race win for a front-engined Ferrari at Monza.

It was clearly to be a Ferrari benefit and the three red cars drew away from the rest of the field from the start in the order of Ginther, Hill and Mairesse. Scarlatti displaced the third Ferrari before the end of the first lap as Mairesse had deliberately dropped back to give von Trips a tow. Soon all four works Ferraris were filling the first four places but their plan was upset when Gino Munaron in a Cooper-Ferrari, (also known as a Cooper-Castellotti,) managed to climb to third place. Then Cabianca, in a second Cooper-Ferrari, overtook him. After pit stops for fuel and tyres, the order became Hill, Ginther, Mairesse, Cabianca, von Trips, with the Porsche's of Herrmann and Barth in 6th and 7th places. It was a very Italian affair, robbed of much interest by the British boycott and it was also the swan song of the front engined Ferraris. **Phil Hill won at 132.062 mph**, with Ginther 2nd and Mairesse 3rd but Cabianca's Cooper-Ferrari finished ahead of von Trips. The fastest lap of the race was recorded by Phil Hill at 136.731 mph.

United States Grand Prix: November 20

The British contingent was back in force for the last race of the Season at Riverside while this time it was the Ferraris that stayed away. Phil Hill joined Olivier Gendebien, Tony Brooks and Henry Taylor in driving Yeoman Credit Coopers, all but Henry Taylor having cars with Colotti gearboxes and high tails. Wolfgang von Trips drove a Cento Sud Cooper-Maserati and Ron Flockhart was on the back row of the grid in 21st place driving a third works Cooper-Climax. Stirling Moss took pole position with Rob Walker's Lotus-Climax from Jack Brabham (Cooper-Climax), Dan Gurney (B.R.M.) Joakim Bonnier (B.R.M.) and Jim Clark (Lotus-Climax).

After the start it was Brabham, Moss and Gurney and this order remained unchanged as, behind them, Surtees spun and collected Clark. Then a fire caused by an overfilled fuel tank delayed Brabham, and Moss led comfortably from Gurney who retired with overheating on lap 18. Bonnier dropped back with a rough sounding engine and **Stirling Moss won the race at 99.00 mph** from Innes Ireland (Lotus-Climax) Bruce McLaren (Cooper-Climax) Brabham (Cooper-Climax) and Bonnier (B.R.M.). The fastest lap was set by Brabham, who had been on a charge after his fire, at 101.38 mph.

The World Championship

Jack Brabham won the World Championship for the second year running with 43 points, Bruce McLaren was second with 34. Stirling Moss had 19, Innes Ireland 18, Phil Hill 16, both Olivier Gendebien and Wolfgang von Trips 10, and Ritchie Ginther, Jim Clark, and Tony Brooks shared 10th place with 8 points each.

The Constructors Championship was even more emphatically won by Cooper-Climax with 48 points. Lotus-Climax scored 34, Ferrari 26, B.R.M. 8, Cooper-Maserati 3 and Cooper-Ferrari 3.

NON CHAMPIONSHIP RACES

The German Grand Prix

It had been decided that the 1960 German Grand Prix should be for Formula 2 cars which meant that a German car was likely to win and also that the race would probably be dull. Wet conditions didn't improve things and in addition Enzo Ferrari chose to withdraw his entries. Bonnier (F2 Porsche) gained pole position in practice, von Trips (F2 Porsche) was second, and Jack Brabham (Cooper-Climax) third.

In a race which "Motor Sport" described as being "wet and miserable" Bonnier led from the start followed by von Trips, Brabham and Herrmann (Porsche). Graham Hill managed to overtake Herrmann in yet another Porsche and they finished in that order.

Joakim Bonnier winning the non World Championship German Grand Prix for Formula 2 cars.

The BRDC International Trophy Race

Sadly the popular driver Harry Schell was killed in practice when his Cooper crashed into a marker wall. Stirling Moss was fastest in practice for this 150 mile race in Rob Walker's Cooper-Climax and then came Joakim Bonnier and Dan Gurney in B.R.Ms and Phil Hill's Ferrari.

Innes Ireland (Lotus-Climax) being followed by Stirling Moss (Cooper-Climax) while lapping Keith Green's Cooper-Maserati during the International Trophy Race at Silverstone.

Bonnier led from the start of the race, followed by Gurney, Graham Hill (B.R.M.) and Moss, but by the beginning of the second lap Moss was out in front and behind him came Bonnier, Gurney and Innes Ireland (Lotus-Climax). On lap 7 Moss broke the lap record at 110.917 mph but was being pressed hard by Ireland. Then on lap 33 the suspension broke on Rob Walker's Cooper and so the race was won by Ireland, followed by Jack Brabham Cooper-Climax) and Graham Hill.

The Monte Carlo Rally

The 1960 Monte Carlo Rally was dominated by the Mercedes Benz 220SEs which finished in first, second, third and fifth places, the winning car being driven by Walter Schock and Rolf Moll. Ford had 39 entries and Sunbeam 28. Amongst other British

The winning Mercedes Benz 220 SE during the 1960 Monte Carlo Rally.

manufacturers were Austin, Triumph, Riley, Singer, Wolesley, Hillman, M.G. and Morgan. It was when Great Britain still had a formidable motor industry. Sunbeam scored a Class win. Schock and Moll also won the 1960 European Championship.

Targa Florio

There were Ferraris for Allison/Phil Hill, von Trips/Ginther, Mairesse/Scarfiotti, Cabianca and the Rodriguez brothers in Sicily for the 1960 Targa Florio. Porsche brought a RS60 car for Barth/Graham Hill, and two further RS60s for Bonnier, Herrmann and Gendebien. Von Hanstein/Pucci had a Porsche Carrera. Maserati was represented by a Camoradi Tipo 61 for Maglioli/Vaccarella to drive.

As usual smaller cars started first but at the end of the first lap the order was Bonnier, Maglioli, Gendebien with the Ferraris of Allison, Mairesse and von Trips next up. As the race settled down with stops for fuel and driver changes the order became Maglioli/Vaccarella (Maserati), Bonnier/Herrman (Porsche), Gendebien (Porsche) and von Trips/Phil Hill (Ferrari). Colin Davis had been going well in a Cooper-Maserati but retired with a broken header tank. Then the Maglioli/Vaccarella Maserati's race ended when with a punctured tank it ran out of fuel, and Vaccarella, coasting out of gear crashed into a bank. The Bonnier/Herrmann Porsche inherited the lead which it maintained to the end. The von Trips/Phil Hill Ferrari was 2nd, the Gendebien/Herrmann Porsche 3rd and the Barth/Graham Hill Porsche 4th.

Le Mans

The 3 litre V12 Ferrari of Frere/Gendebien won the Le Mans 24 Hour Race with an unchallenged lead after the first hour and an average speed of 109.19 mph. Another 3 litre Ferrari entered by N.A.R.T (North American Racing Team) and driven by Ricardo

Olivier Gendebien about to embark on a further stint in his Ferrari to win the 1960 Le Mans 24 Hour race.

The Rambaux/Boutin AC Ace Bristol which retired in the 14th hour at Le mans with a broken piston.

Rodriguez/Pilette was second. An Aston Martin DB1/300 entered by Border Reviers and driven by Clark/Salvadori finished third at an average speed of 106.61 mph. Ferrari G.Ts finished in fourth, fifth, sixth and seventh places and then came the Chevrolet Corvette entered by Briggs Cunningham and driven by Fitch/Grossman. The two other works Ferraris of von Trips/Phil Hill and Scarfiotti/Pedro Rodriguez both retired when they ran out of fuel. Briggs Cunningham's works prepared E2A Type Jaguar, driven by Hansgen/Gurney was delayed with a fuel leak and eventually retired with engine trouble after being involved to two collisions in the tenth hour. The Aston Martin DBR1 which had won in 1959 was privately entered and driven by Baillie/Fairman to finish in 9th place after losing an hour while stuck in a sand bank. Other British entries included A.C Ace Bristols, an Austin Healey 3000 driven by Sears/Riley, a D Type Jaguar driven by Flockhart/Halford, numerous Lotus Elites, one of which was driven by Masson/Lautent Wagstaff/Marsh to finish 13th, and another, driven by Wagstaff/Marsh finished in 14th place. The M.G.A of Lund/Escott finished in 12th place but three works entered Triumph TR4s failed to be placed because they had covered insufficient mileage.

The Lund/Escott MGA which was placed 12th after completing 2188.70 miles at an average speed of 91.20 mph.

1961
Little cars with great hearts

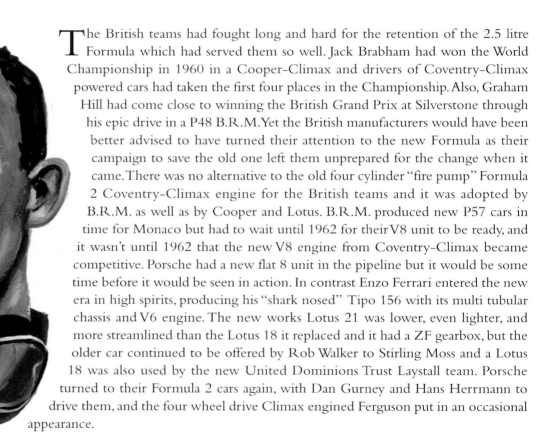

Stirling Moss.

The British teams had fought long and hard for the retention of the 2.5 litre Formula which had served them so well. Jack Brabham had won the World Championship in 1960 in a Cooper-Climax and drivers of Coventry-Climax powered cars had taken the first four places in the Championship. Also, Graham Hill had come close to winning the British Grand Prix at Silverstone through his epic drive in a P48 B.R.M. Yet the British manufacturers would have been better advised to have turned their attention to the new Formula as their campaign to save the old one left them unprepared for the change when it came. There was no alternative to the old four cylinder "fire pump" Formula 2 Coventry-Climax engine for the British teams and it was adopted by B.R.M. as well as by Cooper and Lotus. B.R.M. produced new P57 cars in time for Monaco but had to wait until 1962 for their V8 unit to be ready, and it wasn't until 1962 that the new V8 engine from Coventry-Climax became competitive. Porsche had a new flat 8 unit in the pipeline but it would be some time before it would be seen in action. In contrast Enzo Ferrari entered the new era in high spirits, producing his "shark nosed" Tipo 156 with its multi tubular chassis and V6 engine. The new works Lotus 21 was lower, even lighter, and more streamlined than the Lotus 18 it replaced and it had a ZF gearbox, but the older car continued to be offered by Rob Walker to Stirling Moss and a Lotus 18 was also used by the new United Dominions Trust Laystall team. Porsche turned to their Formula 2 cars again, with Dan Gurney and Hans Herrmann to drive them, and the four wheel drive Climax engined Ferguson put in an occasional appearance.

THE WORLD CHAMPIONSHIP SEASON

Monaco Grand Prix: May 14

The first World Championship race turned out to be one of the all time greats and it firmly established the new 1.5 litre Formula in the hearts and minds of every enthusiast by confounding all its critics. As soon as the first practice commenced in Monaco it became clear that the new V6 Ferraris would not have it all their own way. A crash on the first day limited Jim Clark's time with the new Lotus 21 but he had already put in a time which proved to be fast enough to secure a place on the front row of the grid. Stirling Moss was fastest of all in Rob Walker's Lotus 18 and, between them, enjoying an extra 30 bhp, was Richie Ginther's Ferrari Next came Graham Hill (B.R.M-Climax) and Phil Hill (Ferrari). The third row consisted of Wolfgang von Trips (Ferrari) Bruce McLaren (Cooper-Climax) and Tony Brooks (B.R.M-Climax). Innes Ireland (Lotus-Climax) had also crashed during practice and, having sustained a broken leg, became a spectator.

Ritchie Ginther's Ferrari being chased by Stirling Moss' Lotus-Climax during the early stages of the Monaco Grand Prix .

A painting of the Tipo 156 Ferrari at Monaco which Phil Hill had framed and hung in his home in Santa Monica.

Ginther was first away at the fall of the flag and immediately established a useful lead from Clark, Moss, Gurney (Porsche) and Brooks. Clark, whose car had been smoking at the start, came into his pit for repairs. He subsequently dropped back through the field with electrical problems. Then Moss set about catching the flying Ferrari and behind him was Bonnier (Porsche) and Brooks (B.R.M-Climax). Both Moss and Bonnier overtook Ginther on lap 14 but then it was Phil Hill who led the Italian attack. At 40 laps Moss had a 10 second lead over Phil Hill but Ginther was determined to pass his team mate and resume his battle for the lead. He achieved this on lap 70 but, in spite of his power deficit, Moss held on to his lead, taking full advantage of the traffic as the two cars lapped most of the field, including von Trips' Ferrari. Bonnier had retired as had both Graham Hill and Brooks, and **Moss crossed the finishing line 3.6 seconds ahead of Ginther to win at a speed of 70.704 mph.** Phil Hill was 3rd, von Trips 4th but 2 laps behind. Ginther and Moss both achieved the fastest lap of the race at 73.054 mph. By comparison the fastest lap in 1960 with the 2.5 litre Formula had been 73.131 mph!

Dutch Grand Prix: May 22

Ferraris, now with improved 120 degree V6 engines which produced 190 bhp, filled the front row of the grid at Zandvoort in the order of Phil Hill, Wolfgang von Trips and Richie Ginther. Moss had to choose between Rob Walker's Cooper and Lotus and decided to opt for the Lotus with the improved 4 cylinder Coventry-Climax engine which produced 150 bhp. Trevor Taylor drove Innes Ireland's works Lotus as Ireland hadn't recovered from his crash at Monaco. Dan Gurney had a Porsche with a lengthened chassis. Behind the three Ferraris on the starting grid were Stirling Moss (Lotus-Climax) and Graham Hill (B.R.M-Climax). Jim Clark was back in 10th place in his Lotus-Climax and Taylor was on the back row in 14th position.

Opposite: Stirling Moss on his way to his memorable win at Monaco in 1961 driving Rob Walker's Lotus 18.

The Ferraris of Wolfgang von Trips and Phil Hill leading the Dutch Grand Prix at Zandvoort.

At the start it was von Trips who seized an early lead from Phil Hill, the two managing to squeeze Moss out. Ginther was held back with excessive wheel spin so it was Graham Hill and Clark who were not far behind the leading pair. Clark eventually overtook the B.R.M. before setting about Phil Hill's Ferrari while Graham Hill dropped further back after a spin. It became clear that Phil Hill was defending von Trips' lead by holding Clark back, and this resulted in the two cars being side by side on a number of occasions. Eventually Phil Hill detached himself from Clark and caught his team mate up and that was how the race ended. Both Clark and Moss stayed ahead of Ginther in 5th place and Clark established the fastest lap of the race at 98.214 mph. **Von Trips' winning speed was 96.205 mph.**

Belgian Grand Prix June 18

The red Ferraris of Phil Hill and Wolfgang von Trips together with the yellow Ferrari of the Belgian Olivier Gendebien filled the front row of the starting grid at Spa. Then came John Surtees (Cooper-Climax) and the fourth Ferrari of Richer Ginther. The third row consisted of the Coventry-Climax engined B.R.Ms of Graham Hill and Tony Brooks and the Lotus-Climax of Stirling Moss. Jim Clark was back in 18th place. Cliff Allison was involved in an accident during practice when he was thrown out of his U.D.T-Laystall Lotus-Climax and sustained serious leg injuries.

Graham Hill came through from the second row to lead the race at the start but before the end of the first lap he was overtaken by all four Ferraris. Gendebien's car, being entered for Ferrari by Equipe Belge, had an earlier 65 degree V6 Monaco engine but was holding third place behind von Trips and Phil Hill. Throwing caution to the wind he actually led the race on his home ground for a couple of laps in his less powerful car before slowing to conserve his engine and to settle for fourth place. John Surtees (Cooper-Climax) then disputed fifth place with Graham Hill, giving the crowd something to get excited about until the B.R.M. was forced to pit on lap 19 with a split exhaust pipe and burnt plug leads. He eventually retired on lap 24 with an oil leak. **Phil Hill won the race at 128.148 mph** from von Trips, Ginther and Gendebien The Ferraris were followed across the line by Surtees (Cooper-Climax), Dan Gurney (Porsche) and Moss Lotus-Climax). Ginther set the fastest lap at 131.529 mph in catching up with the two leading Ferraris. Clark finished in 12th place six laps behind the Ferraris.

French Grand Prix: July 2

It was no surprise that the front row of the starting grid at Rheims consisted of the Ferraris of Phil Hill, Wolfgang von Trips and Richie Ginther. A fourth Ferrari, which had been loaned to a group of Italian motor racing clubs, was driven by Giancarlo Baghetti into 12th place on the grid. The three works Ferraris had gauze covers for their carburettors in place of the Perspex ones and Ginther experimented with a high streamlined air intake above his head rest. Stirling Moss (Lotus-Climax) who had artfully managed to obtain a tow in the slip stream of von Trips Ferrari, was 4th in practice ahead of Jim Clark (Lotus-Climax), Graham Hill (B.R.M.), John Surtees (Cooper-Climax) and Bruce McLaren (Cooper-Climax).

The order on the first lap of the race was Phil Hill, Ginther, von Trips, Moss and Surtees. Then Moss overtook Ginther when he spun but, in successfully avoiding Ginther's spinning Ferrari, Surtees damaged his suspension on a bank and was forced to retire. Von Trips overtook Phil Hill while Moss, slowing with brake trouble, was overtaken by Baghetti, Innes Ireland and Clark. Von Trips retired on lap 18 with engine trouble leaving Phil Hill in the lead with Ginther in second place while Baghetti challenged the Lotus-Climax cars of Ireland and Clark and the F2 Porsche of Dan Gurney. The two Ferraris appeared to be unassailable at the front until Phil Hill spun while lapping Moss. The inevitable contact resulted in Moss' retirement and put the Ferrari driver right out of contention. Then Ginther stopped on lap 41 with low oil pressure so that Baghetti, driving a privately entered Ferrari in his first World Championship race led the race from Gurney, Clark and Ireland. **Baghetti became Italy's new hero when he won at an average speed of 119.846 mph,** the fastest lap of the race being recorded by Phil Hill at 126.247 mph.

British Grand Prix: July 15

There were four Ferraris at Aintree for Phil Hill, Wolfgang von Trips, Richie Ginther and Giancarlo Baghetti. The British teams were still waiting for the new V8 engines from Coventry-Climax and B.R.M, and Porsche was still without its new flat 8. In spite of this the big surprise during practice was the performance of Joakim Bonnier's 4 cylinder Formula 2 Porsche which was on the front row of the starting grid alongside the Ferraris of Phil Hill and Richie Ginther. Jack Fairman drove the four wheel drive Ferguson-Climax which was entered by Rob Walker and finished in his colours. Stirling Moss showed something of the car's potential in practice and Jack Fairman took it to the eighth row of the grid.

Starting Grid

P. Hill	P.R. Ginther	J. Bonnier
Ferrari	Ferrari	Porsche
I min 58.8 secs	1 min 58.8 secs	1 min 58.8 secs

	W. von Trips	S. Moss	
	Ferrari	Lotus-Climax	
	1 min 58.8 secs	1 min 59.0 secs	

C.A.S. Brooks	I. Ireland	J. Clark
B.R.M-Climax	Lotus-Climax	Lotus-Climax
1 min 59.0 secs	1 min 59.2 secs	1 min 59.2 secs

	J. Brabham	J. Surtees	
	Cooper-Climax	Cooper-Climax	
	1 min 59.4 secs	1 min 59.6 secs	

G. Hill	D. Gurney	R. Savadori
B.R.M-Climax	Porsche	Cooper-Climax
2 min 00.0 secs	2 min 00.2 secs	2 min 00.8 secs

	B. McLaren	J. Lewis	
	Cooper-Climax	Cooper-Climax	
	2 min 01.0 secs	2 min 01.0 secs	

M. Gregory	H. Taylor	C.G de Beaufort
Cooper-Climax	Lotus-Climax	Porsche
2 min 01.4 secs	2 min 01.8 secs	2 min 02.0 secs

	G. Baghetti	J. Fairman	
	Ferrari	Ferguson-Climax	
	2 min 02.0 secs	2 min 03.4 secs	

L. Bandini	W. Seidel	K. Greene
Cooper-Maserati	Lotus-Climax	Gilby-Climax
2 min 03.6 secs	2 min 04.2 secs	2 min 06.0 secs

A. Maggs		I. Burgess
Lotus-Climax		Lotus-Climax
2 min 06.4 secs		2 min 06.6 secs
G. Ashmore	A. Marsh	N. Natili
Lotus-Climax	Lotus-Climax	Cooper-Maserati
2 min 08.2 secs	2 min 09.6 secs	2 min 10.2 secs
T. Parnell		L. Bianchi
Lotus-Climax		Lotus-Climax
2 min 16.8 secs		2 min 18.8 secs

Wolfgang von Trips driving his Tipo 156 Ferrari through torrential rain at Aintree.

Stirling Moss showing what the 4 wheel drive Ferguson-Climax could do in the later stages of the British Grand Prix.

The race started in a downpour and, in consequence, wet weather Dunlop tyres were the obvious choice for most of the teams. From the fall of the flag three Ferraris were at the front in the order of Phil Hill, Wolfgang von Trips and Richie Ginther, and they were followed by Stirling Moss, Joakim Bonnier, Graham Hill and Jack Brabham. Then Moss, who had clung to the third Ferrari, moved up into third place when Ginther spun. Behind Ginther were Joakim Bonnier John Surtees, Jim Clark, Tony Brooks and Graham Hill. Then Phil Hill and Moss managed to catch up with von Trips as the German driver was lapping the tail enders, and both of them passed the leading Ferrari on lap 10. Four laps later Moss was actually challenging for the lead when his car began to slide at high speed on the wet circuit. He held the Lotus magnificently as it swooped ends and then continued to motor at unabated speed, still in second place! As the race progressed the rain stopped and von Trips was still leading Moss, Ginther and Phil Hill. Then Moss slowed with failing brakes and eventually retired on lap 45. After this Moss took over the Ferguson-Climax and he put in some impressively quick laps with the car. When the race ended it was an expected Ferrari 1 − 2 − 3 with **Wolfgang von Trips winning at 83.91 mph** from Phil Hill and Ginther. The fastest lap of the race was set by that superlative driver Tony Brooks (B.R.M–Climax) at 91.68 mph.

Results

1.	W. Von Trips Ferrari	2 hr 40 min 53.6 secs
2.	P. Hill Ferrari	2 hr 41 min 39.6 secs
3.	P.R. Ginther Ferrari	2 hr 41 min 40.4 secs
4.	J. Brabham Cooper–Climax	2 hr 42 min 02.2 secs
5.	J. Bonnier Porsche	2 hr 42 min 09.8 secs
6.	R. Salvadori Cooper–Climax	2 hr 42 min 19.8 secs
7.	D. Gurney Porsche	1 lap
8.	B. McLaren Cooper–Climax	
9.	C.A.S Brooks B.R.M–Climax	2 laps
10.	I. Ireland Lotus–Climax	3 laps
11.	M. Gregory Cooper–Climax	4 laps
12.	L. Bandini Cooper–Maserati	
13.	A. Maggs Lotus–Climax	6 laps
14.	I. Burgess Lotus–Climax	
15.	K. Greene Gilby–Climax	
16.	C. G. De Beaufort Porsche	
17.	W. Seidel Lotus–Climax	17 laps

Retirements

M. Natili Cooper-Maserati lap 1 engine

H. Taylor Lotus-Climax lap 6 spun

G. Ashmore Lotus-Climax lap8

T. Parnell Lotus-Climax lap 13 clutch

J. Surtees Cooper-Climax lap 24 crownwheel and pinion

A. Marsh Lotus-Climax lap 26

G. Baghetti Ferrari lap 28 spun

G. Hill B.R.M–Climax lap 44 engine

S. Moss Lotus-Climax lap 45 brake pipe

L. Bianchi Lotus-Climax lap 46 gearbox

J. Fairman/Stirling Moss Ferguson lap 57 disqualified.

J. Clark Lotus-Climax lap 63 oil leak.

German Grand Prix: August 6

The eagerly awaited V8 Coventry-Climax engine arrived at the Nurburgring installed in Jack Brabham's suitably modified works Cooper. Embarrassingly, its distributor driveshaft broke when it was first started up in the paddock, but after this unit was replaced the car was impressive. The starting grid suggested a close race as four makes shared the front row in the order of Phil Hill's Ferrari, Jack Brabham's V8 Cooper-Climax, Stirling Moss' 4 cylinder Lotus-Climax with Colotti gearbox, and Joakim Bonnier's Porsche. Jim Clark was 8th and on the third row of the grid. Three of the Ferraris had 120 degree V6 engines while Giancarlo Baghetti's car still had an earlier 60 degree V6 unit.

The race was started by the great Juan Fangio and it was Brabham who led the field away but he spun off the wet circuit to end his race on the first of the 14 mile laps. It was a great disappointment. The order was then Moss, Phil Hill, Hans Herrmann (Porsche) and Graham Hill (B.R.M-Climax). Graham Hill also left both the circuit and the race abruptly before the end of the first lap after contact with Dan Gurney's Porsche. Wolfgang von Trips (Ferrari) took third place from Hans Herrmann (Porsche) and then second place from Phil Hill. Innes Ireland's Lotus-Climax caught fire but he managed to jump out so as to escape being badly burned. Driving superbly, and recalling his performance in the Monaco Grand Prix, Moss stayed ahead of Phil Hill, von Trips, Clark (Lotus-Climax) and John Surtees (Cooper-Climax), in spite of his car being shod with rain tyres in drying conditions, while Tony Brooks (B.R.M-Climax) retired on lap 7 with engine trouble. Extending his lead when it started to rain again, **Stirling Moss won the race at 92.297 mph** from the Ferraris of von Trips and Phil Hill. Clark was 4th, Surtees 5th, and Bruce McLaren (Cooper-Climax) 6th. The fastest lap went to Phil Hill at 94.876 mph.

Tony Brooks driving the Climax engine P57 B.R.M. on the Nurburgring.

Italian Grand Prix: September 10

This time the British teams agreed to race at Monza in spite of the inclusion of the banked section of the circuit. In addition to Jack Brabham, Stirling Moss also had a V8 Coventry-Climax engine, fitted in Rob Walker's Lotus which had been extensively modified to receive it. B.R.M. brought two brand new V8 cars in addition to their well tried Coventry-Climax engined models but, although the new cars performed well, it was decided to use the earlier cars in the race. Moss experienced some trouble with the V8 Lotus and was given a 4 cylinder works Lotus fitted with upper body panels in Rob Walker blue. Its lower panels remained green and its wheels yellow! The Ferraris of Wolfgang von Trips and Ricardo Rodriguez were on the front row of the grid, the latter having the earlier 60 degrees engine. Then came the Ferraris of Richie Ginther and Phil Hill, followed by Graham Hill's B.R.M-Climax and Giancarlo Baghetti's Ferrari. Brabham and Moss were only 9th and 10th.

Graham Hill and Jim Clark got amongst the Ferraris on the first lap but the banked section of the circuit enabled the Ferraris of Phil Hill and the Mexican Rodriguez to stamp their authority on the race. Clark and Brabham still headed von Trips at the end of the lap and then tragedy struck when Wolfgang von Trips's Ferrari and Clark's Lotus collided. Von Trips was flung out of his car as the car mounted a bank at great speed and then spun back across the track, killing the driver and eleven spectators. Fortuitously Clark survived the crash uninjured but his car was wrecked. On lap 2 the order was Phil Hill, Ginther, Rodriguez, Baghetti and Brabham, the V8 Coventry-Climax engine alone being able to stay with the Ferraris. Behind Brabham Moss, while was falling back 2 while leading the pack. Brabham retired on lap 9 with an overheating engine and the four Ferraris continued to lead. Then on lap 14 both Rodriguez and Giancarlo Baghetti retired with engine failures while Phil Hill and Ginther continued to circulate at the front followed, at a distance, by Moss and Gurney's Porsche. Ginther's was the next Ferrari to retire, with engine trouble on lap 24, and Moss was eliminated with a broken wheel bearing on lap 37. The sad race ended with **Phil Hill winning at 130.107 mph** from Gurney's Porsche and Bruce McLaren's Cooper-Climax. The fastest lap was set by Baghetti at 132.834 mph.

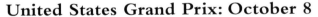

Wolfgang von Trips

United States Grand Prix: October 8

The United States Grand Prix took place at Watkins Glen in 1962, the date having been brought forward to avoid the snow. Following the death of "Taffy" von Trips at Monza the Ferrari team stayed at home but Jack Brabham was there with a V8 Cooper-Climax and Stirling Moss with Rob Walker's V8 Lotus-Climax. Both also had the option of cars with 4 cylinder engines. B.R.M. left their new V8 cars at Bourne for further development work and so Graham Hill and Tony Brooks persevered with the 4 cylinder Climax engined P57s. Olivier Gendebien had a major crash during practice in his U.D.T-Laystall Lotus-Climax but he was uninjured and his car was repaired in time for the race. Brabham won pole position with Graham Hill alongside him in the B.R.M-Climax. Moss was in the second row with the 4 cylinder Lotus, having made the second fastest time with the V8 engined car. Bruce McLaren was 4th in practice with his 4 cylinder Cooper-Climax, Jim Clark 5th in his Lotus-Climax and Innes Ireland was 10th in his Lotus.

Brabham led initially but by the end of the first lap the order was Moss, Brabham, Ireland up from the fourth row of the grid, and Graham Hill. Bruce McLaren improved his position to 3rd place while Ireland spun and dropped to 11th. Seven laps later Ireland was up to 4th place again! On lap 6 Brabham was back in the lead, hotly pursued by Moss, while Walt Hansgen's Cooper-Climax developed a fire in its engine compartment which extinguished itself a few laps later! Moss recovered the lead on lap 16 and he and Brabham swopped places more than once for a number of laps. Behind these two were McLaren (Cooper-Climax), Ireland (Lotus-Climax) and Graham Hill (B.R.M-Climax). Jim Clark's Lotus-Climax slowed with a failing clutch and Brabham dropped back to retire with engine trouble on lap 58, leaving Moss clearly in the lead from Ireland. McLaren had fallen away with gearbox problems and on lap 59 it was Moss who had to pull out of the race altogether with a blown engine. Roy Salvadori (Cooper-Climax) was now second to Ireland and closing on him until the engine of his Yeoman Credit Cooper expired on lap 95. **So the last race of the Season went to Innes Ireland at a speed of 103.17 mph.** It was the first win by Lotus in a World Championship race. The fastest lap of the race was made by Brabham at 105.88 mph. Dan Gurney (Porsche) was second and Tony Brooks (B.R.M-Climax) was third. It would prove to be Tony Brooks' last World Championship race.

The World Championship

Phil Hill won the World Championship with 34 points. Wolfgang von Trips was second with 33 and Stirling Moss third with 21. Dan Gurney also had 21 points, Richie Ginther 16, Innes Ireland 12, Jim Clark and Bruce McLaren 11, Giancarlo Baghetti 9, Tony Brooks 6, Jack Brabham and John Surtees 4, Olivier Gendebien, Jack Lewis, Joakim Bonnier and Graham Hill 3 and Roy Salvadori 2.

The Constructors' World Championship went to Ferrari with 40 points. Lotus-Climax had 32, Porsche 22, Cooper-Climax 14 and B.R.M-Climax 7.

The Solitude Grand Prix

Apart from Ferrari and B.R.M. all the main teams came to Solitude and Porsche arrived with four 4 cylinder cars for its three drivers, Joakim Bonnier, Dan Gurney, Hans Herrmann. Bonnier won pole position in practice and was followed by Gurney Porsche), Innes Ireland (B.R.P-Climax), Stirling Moss (Lotus-Climax), Hans Herrmann (Porsche), and Jim Clark (Lotus-Climax).

Innes Ireland winning the Solitude Grand Prix in the B.R.P.-Climax. Innes later told me that Bonnier was not at all thrilled at being beaten on Porsches home ground. He also said that the B.R.P. car was based on the Lotus 25 but didn't handle nearly as well.

Ireland led from the start, followed by Bruce McLaren (Cooper-Climax), Herrmann and Gurney. As the race progressed Ireland was closely followed by Bonnier and Gurney, while neither Moss nor Clark was amongst the leaders. Bonnier passed Ireland on the penultimate lap but Ireland heroically went by on the grass after leaving his braking very late on the last lap. He won by just three feet from Bonnier who was followed by Gurney, McLaren and Brabham (Cooper-Climax).

The South African Grand Prix

In "All my races" Stirling Moss records that he spent Christmas Eve in 1961 teaching Jim Clark to water ski. On Boxing Day they both took part in the South African Grand Prix in East London. Clark (Lotus-Climax) was fastest in practice with Moss (UDT Laystall Lotus-Climax) 2nd, Trevor Taylor (Lotus-Climax) 3rd, Joakim Bonnier (Porsche) 4th, Masten Gregory (UDT Laystall Lotus-Climax) 5th, and Tony Maggs (Cooper-Climax) 6th. Moss was overtaken by the two works Lotus drivers soon after the start. Taylor retired on lap 3 with a holed radiator and Clark, after spinning, recovered his lead to win from Moss, with Bonnier finishing 3rd and Maggs 4th.

Stirling Moss on his way to second place in Rob Walker's Lotus 18/21 in British Racing Partnership colours in the South African Grand Prix.

The Monte Carlo Rally

Panhards came first, second and third in the 1961 Monte Carlo Rally and the British competitors were furious, believing that the new regulations were biased in a way that assisted the little French cars. All the entries were graded according to their weight and engine capacity but not their power. It favoured the Panhards since they were both small

Andersson/Lohmander Volvo encountering the effects of heavy snow during the 1961 Monte Carlo Rally.

and relatively powerful and they were the favourites to win long before the event was held. In spite of this Ford, Sunbeam, Austin and Morris all entered works teams and the B.B.C. competed with a London Taxi in the hands of Tony Brooks and Peter Dimmock. The weather played its part with an abundance of snow and ice which caught several competitors out on the mountainous roads to Monte Carlo. The highest placed British car was a Sunbeam Rapier driven by Harper and Proctor which came 12th. Another Rapier driven by Hopkirk and Scott finished in 13th place.

Targa Florio

Ferrari had two Tipo 246 mid engined cars for Phil Hill/Gendebien and von Trips/ Ginther with 2.4 litre V6 engines, and a front engined V12 for Ricardo Rodriguez/ Mairesse. Porsche had three RS61 cars for Bonnier/Gurney, Herrmann/Barth and Moss. Graham Hill. There were also two works supported 2.9 litre mid engined Tipo 63 Maseratis for Maglioli/Scarlatti and Vaccarella/Trintignant. Starting at 7 00 a.m the cars were let off at 30 minute intervals, the smallest going first and the Phil Hill/Gendebien Ferrari last of

Wolfgang von Trips passing a Fiat at speed before winning the 1961 Targa Florio.

all. The classic race consisted of ten 44 mile laps across mountains and through towns and villages on public roads, and it was Moss who made the running for the first four laps, the 2 litre silver Porsche having a yellow bonnet to make it clearly seen as it approached the slower cars. Both Moss and Bonnier were breaking the lap record but Gendebien began to overhaul the two Porsches when their co drivers took over and the Ferrari was soon in the lead. Gendebien made an unscheduled stop at an emergency station to take on enough fuel to finish the race but then, responding to the signals of his pit crew, stopped again for von Trips to take the wheel. Moss was now leading once more and he set a new lap record in making good his advantage. Then, sadly, his differential broke putting paid to his race. The von Trips/Gendebien Ferrari won and the Bonnier/Gurney Porsche came second. Third was the Herrmann/Barth Porsche and fourth the Vaccarella/Trintignant Maserati. It was another outstanding race by Stirling Moss which would have been his for the asking had it not been for mechanical failure.

Le Mans

In 1961 Ferrari won the Le Mans 24 Hour race for the fifth year running when the Phil Hill/Gendebien V12 2.9 litre car completed 2781.62 miles at an average speed of 115.90 mph. The four works Ferraris consisted of another front engined 2.9 litre car and two rear engined V6 2.4 litre models. Briggs Cunningham brought along two rear engined Tipo 63 Maseratis and a front engined 2 litre Tipo 60 car. There were eleven Ferraris amongst the entries in all, including a new 250GT which was entered by N.A.R.T and driven by Moss/Graham Hill. It was running in third place after several hours until the fan broke, severing its radiator hose. A dark blue Aston Martin DBR1 entered by Border Reivers and driven by Flockhart/Clark led the race initially in Jim Clark's hands but eventually retired with a failed clutch after a spirited drive. A further Aston Martin DBR1 driven by Salvadori/Maggs retired with a leaking fuel tank after running in 4th. Three Aston Martin DB4 GT Zagatos failed to finish, as did an Austin-Healey 3000 and two Austin-Healey Sprites. An A.C. Ace Bristol finished in 17th place driven by Magne/Alexandrovitch. Lotus Elites finished in 12th and 13th places and the three works Triumph TR4s finished in 9th, 11th and 15th places.

Second overall was the V12 Ferrari of Parkes/Mairesse; 3rd the 250 GT Ferrari of Noblet/Guichet, 4th the V12 Maserati Tipo 63 of Thompson/Pabst and 5th the Porsche RS Coupe driven by Holbert/Gregory.

1962

B.R.M. achieves its founder's dream

The British teams entered the 1962 Season in good heart, with B.R.M. having sufficiently developed its powerful V8 engine for use in new Mark III P57s, and Coventry-Climax being in a position to offer its new V8 to the other teams. At the beginning of the year Colin Chapman produced the Lotus 24 with a multi tubular space frame for his customers and, more importantly, the trend setting Lotus 25 for his works team. Following aircraft design, the Lotus 25 had a monocoque chassis instead of a space frame and this gave it greater rigidity with less weight. Its drivers lay even further back than in the Lotus 18 and, powered by the V8 Coventry-Climax engine, the car instantly proved its worth, eventually persuading all the other teams to opt for monocoques too.

Tony Rudd had been warned by Sir Alfred Owen that a significant number of wins was essential in 1962 if B.R.M. was to have any future beyond the end of the year. Raymond Mays wrote to me before the beginning of the Season to say that there was great optimism in Bourne regarding the new car, and long standing B.R.M. enthusiasts such as myself dared to believe that this could be its year at last.

Graham Hill

A new car entered Formula 1 in 1962 called the Lola-Climax, financed by Bowmaker-Yeoman and managed by Reg Parnell. It was designed by Eric Broadley and had a conventional space frame with wishbone, radius rod suspension at both ends, and a 5 speed Colotti gearbox. The team's drivers were to be John Surtees and Roy Salvadori. Later in 1962, Jack Brabham, following his success with Cooper, decided to produce his own car, with a multi tubular space frame designed by Ron Tauranac and a V8 Coventry-Climax engine. John Cooper, who was not amused, hoped to build upon his success with a refined model that was similar but lighter than his 1961 cars and had a new six speed gearbox.

With the proliferation of Coventry-Climax engined cars, the B.R.M. was alone amongst the British entrants in having its own engine, but Porsche also had a new car with the flat eight air cooled Porsche engine and a six speed gearbox.

Enzo Ferrari, having overwhelmed the opposition in 1961, knew that the Tipo 156 would be much more severely tested in 1962. His cars had been little changed in the course of the winter largely due to the departure, after a disagreement, of Romolo Tavoni, the Team Manager and some key members of his staff. Such modifications that had been carried out on the cars were mainly concerned with the car's road holding. It had been agreed that a Tipo 156, finished in Rob Walker's colours, would be made available for Stirling Moss, but sadly this couldn't happen because of Stirling's appalling accident at Goodwood on Easter Monday in a Lotus-Climax. Thankfully Moss survived the accident, ultimately making a complete recovery, and he would take to the wheel again. Yet his loss to the World Championship Series was universally regretted and represented the end of an era.

THE WORLD CHAMPIONSHIP SEASON

Dutch Grand Prix: May 20

All the new cars apart from the Brabhams arrived in Zandvoort for this first event in the calendar and everyone was anxious to see how they would perform. John Surtees was to drive for the new Lola team and he gained pole position on the grid in his lone Bowmaker Yeoman Lola with a V8 Coventry-Climax engine, having put in a time of 1 min 32.5 secs. Graham Hill was just 0.1 sec slower in the P57 V8 B.R.M. with Lucas Fuel injection, and Jim Clark 0.4 sec slower than him in the brand new V8 monocoque Lotus 25. Jack Brabham was 4th fastest in a Lotus 24, and Bruce McLaren was 5th in the new V8 Cooper-Climax. Richie Ginther, now with B.R.M. was 7th and Phil Hill, Ricardo Rodriguez and Giancarlo Baghetti were only 9th, 11th and 12th in the 120 degree V6 Ferraris. Hill's car had a modified rear suspension and revised gearbox. The works Porsche's were the new 8 cylinder cars with new space frames and 6 speed gearboxes.

Clark made a meteoric start to lead Graham Hill, Gurney (Porsche) who came up from the third row, and Surtees. Rodriguez spun and collected Brabham while Surtees crashed out of the race when his suspension broke. Gurney retired with a gearbox problem and Clark was seriously delayed with clutch trouble. The race was now led by Graham Hill, followed by Bruce McLaren (Cooper-Climax) Phil Hill (Ferrari) and Trevor Taylor in the

Graham Hill winning the Dutch Grand Prix at Zandvoort having established a commanding lead.

second works Lotus-Climax. Then on lap 22 McLaren stopped with gremlins in his gearbox and Taylor overtook Phil Hill. **Graham Hill won the race at 95.439 mph,** Taylor was second, nearly half a minute behind, and then came Phil Hill, Baghetti, Tony Maggs (Cooper-Climax) and Caret Godin de Beaufort (Porsche). Clark finished a lowly 9th, ten laps behind the winner. The fastest lap of the race was achieved by McLaren at 99.358 mph.

Monaco Grand Prix: June 3

Once again the favours were widely distributed amongst the teams in practice at Monaco with five different makes represented by the first five cars on the starting grid. They were in the order of Bruce McLaren (Cooper-V8 Climax) Graham Hill (B.R.M.) Jim Clark (Lotus 25-Climax) Dan Gurney (8 cylinder Porsche) and Willy Mairesse (Ferrari). Joakim Bonnier had a 4 cylinder Porsche and Tony Maggs a 4 cylinder Cooper.

There was mayhem at the start of the race, Mairesse, having bumped both Clark and Graham Hill in coming between the two of them from the second row to gain an initial lead. He proceeded to spin at the hairpin, collecting Richie Ginther (B.R.M.), Dan Gurney (Porsche), Maurice Trintignant (Lotus-Climax), and Innes Ireland (Lotus-Climax). As a result of the wholesale devastation Bruce McLaren led from Graham Hill, Phil Hill, Bonnier and Lorenzo Bandini's Ferrari. Graham Hill passed McLaren while Phil Hill spun his Ferrari, losing both precious seconds and several places. Clark, having rapidly made up ground, passed McLaren to assume second place and go after Graham Hill but, after losing time in passing back markers, his spirited drive came to an end with clutch trouble on lap 56. Brabham, having been running in 3rd place stopped on lap 76 after damaging his suspension in the course of a brief excursion. After this the leading B.R.M. began to emit oil smoke and Hill was robbed of a clear win when his car stopped seven laps from the end. **McLaren won at 70.461 mph,** followed by Phil Hill, Bandini and Surtees (Lola-Climax). The fastest lap was achieved by Jim Clark at 73.666 mph.

An aerial view of the Graham Hill's P57 B.R.M. at Monaco.

Hill's B.R.M. leading the Monaco Grand Prix before an engine failure terminated his race.

Belgian Grand Prix: June 17

Graham Hill put his B.R.M. on pole at Spa and alongside him at the front of the grid were Bruce McLaren (Cooper-Climax) and Trevor Taylor (Lotus-Climax). Masten Gregory had a Lotus-B.R.M. in 8th place with two Ferraris to his left. Jim Clark, his practice having been curtailed by an engine failure, was back in 12th place. Unlike the other Ferraris, that of Ricardo Rodriguez was without an anti roll bar. Ginther's B.R.M. had a 6 speed Colotti gearbox and neither B.R.Ms had the vertical stove pipe exhausts which they had tended to shed in the course of previous races. The two works Coopers of Bruce McLaren and Tony Maggs had V8 Coventry-Climax engines.

Graham Hill took an early lead from McLaren (Cooper-Climax), Trevor Taylor (Lotus-Climax), and Willy Mairesse (Ferrari) with Jim Clark keeping a watching brief already up in 5th place. Taylor led at the end of lap 2 and Graham Hill had dropped to 4th place but

Jim Clark winning his first World Championship race at Spa in his Lotus 25.

The Tipo 156 Ferraris of Ricardo Rodriguez and Phil Hill during the Belgian Grand Prix.

the leading group of cars kept in close company and by lap 8 Clark had moved up to 2nd place before taking the lead on lap 9. After this Clark drew away from Taylor and the rest while Taylor and Mairesse constantly disputed second place. This continued until lap 26 when the Lotus and Ferrari touched at 100 mph, the Lotus burying itself in a ditch and the Ferrari overturning and catching fire. Fortunately both drivers avoided serious injury by being thrown out. **Clark won at an average speed of 131.895 mph** from Graham Hill whose B.R.M. had been slowing with a misfiring engine. Phil Hill was 3rd and he was followed by Rodriguez, John Surtees and Jack Brabham. Clark also established the fastest lap of the race at 133.873 mph.

French Grand Prix: July 8

An industrial dispute had kept Porsche from Spa and Ferrari had to miss Rouen for a similar reason. Porsche had two of their horizontally opposed 8 cylinder cars, modified with stiffened suspension and lowered seats, for Dan Gurney and Joakim Bonnier. Lotus had a new Type 25 monocoque for Jim Clark, and B.R.M. arrived with its own gearboxes for Graham Hill and Richie Ginther in place of Colotti boxes and the cars that were without anti roll bars. Jo Siffert had a works Lotus 24 with a V8 B.R.M. engine. Graham Hill (B.R.M.) and Bruce McLaren (Cooper-Climax) made up the front row of the starting grid and those who had originally opposed the 1.5 litre Formula 1 were beginning to eat their words! Practice resulted in a front row of Jim Clark (Lotus-Climax) Graham Hill (B.R.M.) and Bruce McLaren (Cooper-Climax.) Behind them came Jack Brabham (Lotus-Climax) and John Surtees (Lola-Climax.) Ginther stalled just before the start and Graham Hill led from Surtees, who came through from the second row and was followed by Clark, McLaren and Brabham (Lotus-Climax). Surtees held on to Hill, sometimes getting alongside him, and these two drew away from the rest. Jo Siffert (Lotus-B.R.M.) retired with clutch trouble and McLaren dropped back with gear selection difficulties. At the front Graham Hill broke the lap record at 106.896 mph, underlining the fact that these little cars were capable of lapping more quickly than those of the 2.5 litre Formula had ever done. He was far ahead of Clark when the rear of his B.R.M. was struck by Jack Lewis' Cooper-Climax which he had just lapped. This let Clark and Gurney through but, after Hill had closed on Clark once more, the Lotus driver brought his new car into his pit, unhappy with its performance. The order then became Hill, Gurney, Surtees, but on lap 42 Graham Hill stopped with a fuel injection failure. And

Dan Gurney, a surprised winner of the French Grand Prix at Rouen in his 8 cylinder Porsche.

after this Surtees stopped at his pit with gear box problems. Gurney became the surprise winner from Tony Maggs (Cooper-Climax) and Ginther (B.R.M.). The excitement was still not over as the French police blocked Surtees, who had got going again, as he was entering his pit. This resulted in Trevor Taylor colliding with Maurice Trintignant's Lotus in his efforts to avoid the Lola. Both Lotus-Climax cars were destroyed but mercifully the drivers escaped serious injury. **Dan Gurney's winning speed was 103.225 mph.** Maggs (Cooper-Climax) came 2nd and Richie Ginther (B.R.M.) 3rd. The fastest lap of the race was recorded by Graham Hill at 106.896 mph.

British Grand Prix: July 21

Only one Ferrari came to Aintree. It had a 1961 engine and Phil Hill found himself back in the 5th row of the grid at the end of practice. Jim Clark was in pole position with the Lotus 25 while, unusually, Graham Hill was only 5th. Hill's engine had blown in practice and a replacement had emptied oil over the circuit. The Season was shaping up into a two cornered fight between Clark and Hill but the British Grand Prix was never kind to B.R.M.

Starting grid

J. Clark	J. Surtees	I. Ireland
Lotus-Climax	Lola-Climax	Lotus-Climax
1 min 53.6 secs	1 min 54.2 secs	1 min 54.4 secs

B. McLaren	G. Hill
Cooper-Climax	B.R.M
1 min 54.6 secs	1 min 54.6 secs

D. Gurney	J. Bonnier	P.R. Ginther
Porsche	Porsche	B.R.M
1 min 54.8 secs	1 min 55.2 secs	1 min 55.2 secs

J. Brabham	T. Taylor
Lotus-Climax	Lotus-Climax
1 min 55.4 secs	1 min 56.0 secs

R. Salvadori	P. Hill	A. Maggs
Lola-Climax	Ferrari	Cooper-Climax
1 min 56.2 secs	1 min 56.2 secs	1 min 57 secs

M. Gregory	J. Lewis
Lotus-Climax	Cooper-Climax
1 min 57.2 secs	1 min 59.4 secs

I. Burgess	C.G. de Beaufort	T. Shelly
Cooper-Climax	Porsche	Lotus-Climax
2 min 00.6 secs	2 min 01.4 secs	2 min 02.4 secs

T. Settember	J. Chamberlain
Emeryson-Climax	Lotus-Climax
2 min 02.4 secs	2 min 03.4 secs

W. Seidel
Lotus-B.R.M
2 min 11.6 secs

The lone Ferrari of Phil Hill struggling in mid field at Aintree until retiring with electrical problems.

Innes Ireland was left on the grid with gearbox trouble as the field streamed away with Jim Clark quickly establishing a clear lead from John Surtees, Dan Gurney, Bruce McLaren, Jack Brabham and Graham Hill. Surtees closed on Clark but was kept firmly in second place, Clark having the situation well in hand. Graham Hill passed Brabham while McLaren passed Gurney, and Bonnier retired with a broken crown wheel and pinion. Thereafter it was a largely uneventful race during which Phil Hill's Ferrari was taken out by ignition problems. **Clark eventually won at 92.25 mph** nearly one minute ahead of Surtees. He closed on Hill's B.R.M. which was almost a lap down, towards the end but seemingly declined to pass it. The fastest lap of the race was achieved by Clark at 93.91 mph.

Results

1. J. Clark	Lotus–Climax	2 hr 26 min 20.8 secs
2. J. Surtees	Lola–Climax	2 hr 27 min 10 secs
3. B. McLaren	Cooper–Climax	2 hr 28 min 05.6 secs
4. G. Hill	B.R.M	2 hr 28 min 17.6 secs
5. J. Brabham	Lotus–Climax	1 lap
6. A. Maggs	Cooper–Climax	
7. M. Gregory	Lotus–Climax	
8. T. Taylor	Lotus–Climax	
9. D. Gurney	Porsche	2 laps
10. J. Lewis	Cooper–Climax	3 laps
11. T. Settember	Emeryson–Climax	4 laps
12. I. Burgess	Cooper–Climax	
13. P.R. Ginther	B.R.M	5 laps
14. C.G. de Beaufort	Porsche	6 laps
15. J. Chamberlain	Lotus–Climax	11 laps
16. I. Ireland	Lotus–Climax	14 laps.

Retirements

T. Shelly Lotus–Climax overheating lap 6
W. Seidel Lotus–B.R.M. brakes and overheating lap 11
J. Bonnier Porsche crownwheel and pinion lap 27
R. Salvadori Lola–Climax ignition lap 35
P. Hill Ferrari ignition lap 47.

German Grand Prix: August 5

An unnecessary and potentially fatal accident took place in practice at the Nurburgring when a television company's camera fell from Carel de Beaufort's Porsche. Graham Hill was unable to avoid hitting it at 140 mph and the resultant damage caused the B.R.M. to spin on its own oil and to leave the circuit at high speed. Tony Maggs followed suit as his Cooper-Climax also spun on the oil but amazingly both drivers were uninjured. Unfazed by the incident, Hill went on to record the second fastest time. The front row of the grid at the Nurburgring consisted of Dan Gurney (Porsche) Graham Hill (B.R.M.) Jim Clark (Lotus-Climax) and John Surtees (Lola-Climax). Ferrari was back with four cars, Phil Hill's being the one he drove at Aintree with its gearbox in front of the rear axle and its clutch behind it. Ricardo Rodriguez had a 1961 car with a 65 degree V6 engine. Jim Clark had the Lotus 25, Trevor Taylor the Lotus 24, and Maurice Trintignant Rob Walker's rebuilt Lotus 24 with a V8 Climax engine. 5th on the grid was the Cooper-Climax of Bruce McLaren, and he was on the second row with Joakim Bonnier (Porsche) and Richie Ginther (B.R.M.). The Ferraris of Ricardo Rodriguez, Phil Hill and Giancarlo Baghetti were only 10th, 12th and 13th. Jack Brabham had his BT3 Brabham-Climax in a lowly 24th place. Rain was a significant feature during practice and was also on Sunday.

Torrential rain delayed the start of the race and when the flag eventually fell Clark was left with a dead engine. Trevor Taylor (Lotus-Climax) crashed on the first lap when a misfire suddenly cleared. It was Gurney's flat 8 Porsche that led Graham Hill's B.R.M. with Phil Hill's Ferrari right up into third place. Then Surtees (Lola-Climax) and Bruce McLaren (Cooper-Climax) passed the Ferrari and Graham Hill slipped past Gurney to lead the race. Meanwhile Phil Hill hung on to his 5th position ahead of Bonnier and Ricardo Rodriguez. Then Graham Hill found Surtees right behind him and the two drove nose to tail for much of the race with the Lola sometimes getting alongside the B.R.M. Clark, recovering from his disastrous start, climbed through the field, driving brilliantly in the rain, until he was lying fourth to Graham Hill, Surtees and Bonnier. He was lapping faster than the leader before he decided to settle for 4th place. The race finished with **Graham Hill (B.R.M.) winning at 80.351 mph,** from Surtees (Lola-Climax), Gurney (Porsche) Clark (Lotus-Climax), McLaren (Cooper-Climax), Rodriguez (Ferrari), and Bonnier (Porsche). The fastest lap was credited to Graham Hill's B.R.M. at 83.346 mph. Jack Brabham had retired on lap 9 with a broken throttle linkage.

Graham Hill's B.R.M. on its way to winning a wet German Grand Prix.

Graham Hill leading a 1 – 2
victory for B.R.M. at Monza.

Italian Grand Prix: September 16

The new flat 8 cylinder Tomaso-OSCA, which was to have been driven by Roberto Lippi, appeared during practice, but after encountering problems, it was withdrawn from the race. The two main protagonists filled the front row in the order of Jim Clark (Lotus-Climax) and Graham Hill (B.R.M.). Richie Ginther (B.R.M.) was third fastest and Bruce McLaren (Cooper–Climax) fourth. The five Ferraris of Willy Mairesse, Ricardo Rodriguez, Phil Hill, Lorenzo Bandini, and Giancarlo Baghetti were 10th, 11th, 15th, 17th and 18th. Jack Brabham was an absentee. During practice the fastest cars broke the lap record held by the 2.5 litre cars.

Clark stole an initial lead from Surtees (Lola-Climax) but by the end of the first lap the order was Graham Hill, Clark, Ritchie Ginther, John Surtees, Bruce McLaren (Cooper-Climax), Joakim Bonnier (Porsche) and Dan Gurney (Porsche). On lap 3 Clark stopped with transmission problems and he finally retired on lap 13. Graham Hill proceeded to establish a lead of 5 seconds from Surtees and Ginther, who constantly changed places, while further back McLaren and Gurney were similarly employed. Then on lap 43 Surtees pulled out of the race with engine trouble and the two B.R.Ms were out on their own. The race for third place captivated the attention of the crowd with Gurney, Bonnier, McLaren, Maggs, Innes Ireland and three Ferraris all in close contention. Eventually Ireland retired with the failure of his front suspension and 3rd place went narrowly to Bruce McLaren ahead of the Ferraris of Mairesse and Baghetti. **It was a famous win for B.R.M, Graham Hill averaging 123.616 mph and Ginther being 29.8 seconds behind him.**

United States Grand Prix: October 7

The race for the World Championship had developed into a duel between Graham Hill and Jim Clark so that all eyes were on them during practice at Watkins Glen. Colin

Chapman brought two monocoque Lotus 25s for Clark and Trevor Taylor. John Surtees had a massive crash when the steering of his Lola -Climax broke and so he had to start on the back row of the grid in Salvadori's car. Clark was fastest and had Richie Ginther's B.R.M. alongside him. Graham Hill was in third place on the second row with Dan Gurney's Porsche. Jack Brabham gained an encouraging 5th place with his Brabham-Climax. Enzo Ferrari had given up on the Season and so his cars remained in Italy.

At the start Clark led Graham Hill while Ginther was in third place and followed by Jack Brabham (Brabham-Climax), Gurney (Porsche) and McLaren (Cooper-Climax). Gurney moved up to get ahead of Ginther while the leading pair seemed to be in a race on their own. Then on lap 12 Graham Hill managed to pass Clark as the two tackled some back markers and Ginther retrieved his third place from Gurney. Seven laps later Clark was back in front and drew away from Hill, but Ginther in the second B.R.M. slowed with gearbox troubles and finally retired on lap 35 with a blown engine. **Clark was able to ease up towards the end to win at a speed of 108.476 mph** nine seconds ahead of Hill. McLaren was 3rd, Brabham 4th and Gurney 5th . The fastest lap of the race was recorded by Clark at 110.400 mph.

South African Grand Prix: December 29

The 1962 World Championship was to be decided in East London and there was a good deal of comment and speculation in the British Press before it took place. Lotus and B.R.M. each had three cars for their two drivers. The works Coopers had Lucas fuel injection and large V shaped radiator cowls. Practice was, as always, crucial and Jim Clark's Lotus-Climax was just 0.3 sec faster than Graham Hill's B.R.M. on the front row of the starting grid. Jack Brabham (Brabham-Climax) and Innes Ireland (Lotus-Climax) were 3rd and 4th and Richie Ginther (B.R.M.) was 7th and on the fourth row.

Like Ferrari, Porsche were absentees and so, with the exception of the Brabham-Climax and Mike Harris' Cooper-Alfa Romeo, which was last but one on the grid, it was an all-British affair. The last car on the starting grid was a 1961 B.R.M. with a V8 engine driven by the South African Bruce Johnstone.

It was Clark who led from Hill at the start, followed by Tony Maggs (Cooper-Climax) John Surtees (Lola-Climax) Bruce McLaren and Richie Ginther (B.R.M.). Clark drew steadily away from Hill at the rate of a second a lap and seemed to have the race and the World Championship in his pocket. Behind them Trevor Taylor stopped on lap 12 with

Jim Clark and Graham Hill line up for the World Championship decider in East London.

transmission trouble and Surtees on lap 27 with a blown engine. Then smoke began to be emitted from Clark's car and he was forced to stop on lap 62. It was found that a 2 inch bolt had dropped out of the rear of his engine causing oil to spray over the exhaust. The race now belonged to Hill and he finished 50 secs ahead of McLaren's Cooper-Climax. Tony Maggs (Cooper-Climax) was 3rd and Jack Brabham (Brabham-Climax) 4th. Ginther finished in 7th place 4 laps behind and Johnstone 9th. six laps in arrears. **Hill's winning speed was 93.570 mph** but the fastest lap went to Clark at 96.350 mph.

The Motor Sport commented that "it is splendid that Sir Alfred Owen's faith in the B.R.M. has at last been justified after former failures and vicissitudes, especially as this all-British car has its own engine, not a proprietary unit, which is in the true tradition of Grand Prix racing." Sir Alfred Owen had already confirmed that B.R.M. had a future after all!

The World Championship

Graham Hill won the World Championship with 42 points and Jim Clark was second with 30. Then Bruce McLaren scored 27, John Surtees 19, Dan Gurney 15, Phil Hill 14, Tony Maggs 13 and Richie Ginther 10.

The Constructors' World Championship was won by B.R.M. with 42 points. Lotus-Climax had 36, Cooper-Climax 29, Lola-Climax 19, Porsche and Ferrari 18, Brabham-Climax 6 and Lotus-B.R.M. 1.

The Non Championship Brussels Grand Prix

The Brussels Grand Prix took place on April 1 in the form of three Heats. B.R.M. brought one car for Graham Hill, a second having been destroyed by fire while being tested near Bourne by Ritchie Ginther. Hill shared the front row with Stirling Moss (Lotus 18/21), Jim Clark (Lotus 25) and Willy Mairesse (Ferrari). After leading initially, Clark's car developed engine trouble the end of the first lap of Heat I and Hill then led from Tony Marsh in a 1961 B.R.M. with a V8 engine. Hill led until the end from Moss, Mairesse and Marsh. In Heat II the two B.R.Ms were left on the starting line with failed starter motors and they were black flagged after being push started. Willy Mairesse won Heats II and III and the Grand Prix overall.

Stirling Moss driving Rob Walker's Lotus 18/21 in the Brussels Grand Prix.

Monte Carlo Rally

In the face of widespread criticism, the regulations were changed for 1962 so as not to unfairly favour the Panhards with their high performance engines. The British also arrived with some potent competitors such as the Mini Coopers and a Cosworth engined Ford Anglia. The weather was less interesting than the previous year, snow and ice being confined to the most southerly part of the route where studs offered a clear advantage. Pat Moss and Ann Wisdom won the Coupe des Dames in their Mini Cooper, after sliding off the road in snow en route but the car that was fastest on the Grand Prix circuit was an Aston Martin DB4. The Rally was won by Carlsson and Haggborn in a Saab. Bohringer and Lang were second in a Mercedes, Hopkirk and Scott third in a Sunbeam and Proctor and Robson fourth in a second Sunbeam.

Targa Florio

Ferrari's entries for the Targa Florio consisted of a 2 litre V6 19SP for Baghetti/Bandini, a 2.5 litre Dino 246 for Mairesse/Rodriguez and a 2.6 litre V8 for Phil Hill/Gendebien. Porsche had two cars with 2 litre horizontally opposed 8 cylinder engines for Bonnier/Gurney and Vaccarella/Graham Hill, and two Porsche Abarth Carreras for Herrmann/Linge and Pucci/Barth. Colin Davis/Abate drove a 3 litre V12 "Birdcage" Maserati. As always the cars were started at intervals, the smallest being first so that it was some time before a pattern began to develop. Mairesse was the actual leader from the start followed by Baghetti but Baghetti dropped to fourth place to have hasty repairs made to the badly crumpled tail of his car. Bandini took over from Baghetti while Mairesse broke the lap record before stopping for Rodriguez to take his place. Rodriguez proceeded to extend their lead while Bandini narrowed the gap between his Ferrari and the Vaccarello/Bonnier Porsche.

As always it was an exciting and demanding race, but the missing ingredient in 1962 was Stirling Moss. Mairesse/Rodriguez won from Baghetti/Bandini. Third was the Vaccarella/Bonnier Porsche, fourth the Scarlatti/Ferraro Ferrari 250GTO.

Le Mans

From the start the lead was vigorously disputed by the V12 4 litre Ferrari of Gendebien/Phil Hill and the 4 litre Aston Martin P212 of Graham Hill/Ginther, promising a memorable race. Graham Hill was in front with the Aston at the end of the first lap and the exciting duel continued lap after lap until eventually Gendebien managed to open up

The 4 litre V8 Maserati driven by Maurice Trintignant and Lucien Bianchi at Le Mans in 1962.

a little distance between the two cars. They were followed after an interval by three 4 litre V8 Maseratis and a rear engined V6 2.4 litre Ferrari. Sadly the Aston Martin was eventually delayed at its pit by trouble with its dynamo and finally retired in the seventh hour when Hill missed a gear and bent a valve. The Maseratis faded and Gendebien/Phil Hill were first challenged and then briefly led by the 2.4 litre Ferrari of Pedro and Ricardo Rodriguez while the V8 rear engined 2.6 litre Ferrari of Baghetti/Scarfiotti lay third. Then, at 4 30 a.m. the Rodriguez Ferrari retired with transmission trouble and the Gendebien/Phil Hill car finally established a sufficient lead to be able to slow towards the end, preserving an engine that was no longer sounding crisp. They completed 2765.86 miles at an average speed of 115.25 mph. Behind them Noblet/Guichet (Ferrari 250 G.T.O) finished 2nd, Elde/Beurlys (Ferrari 250 G.T.O) 3rd and the E Type Jaguars of Cunningham/Salvadori and Lumsden/Sargent 4th and 5th.

The A.C Ace Bristol driven by Magne/Martin retired with clutch trouble after 5 hours, and the Aston Martin DB4 GT Zagatos of Kerguen/Frane and Salmon/Baille both retired in the twelfth hour. An Austin-Healey 3000 driven by Olthoff/Whitmore retired during the ninth hour having been circulating in tenth place, and an E Type Jaguar driven by Charles/Coundley retired in the fourth hour. Lotus Elites driven by Hobbs/Gardner and Hunt/Wyllie finished in 8th and 11th places.

The Sebring 12 Hours Race

Stirling Moss and Innes Ireland shared a Ferrari 250 Testa Rossa and Fulp/Ryan a new V8 Ferrari 248SP. The Rodriguez brothers drove a Ferrari 246SP V6 Dino and Gendebien/Phil Hill a 250 GT Ferrari. The Stirling Moss/Ireland car went into an early lead and held on to it until half distance when their car was black flagged for infringing the regulations. Then the Rodriguez brothers led until mechanical troubles brought their race to a premature end. They took over a privately entered car and led with this until failing oil pressure led to their second retirement in the 10th hour. At the end of the twelve hours the winners were Jo Bonnier and Lucien Bianchi in a Ferrari TR61.

Opposite, top: The Graham Hill/Ritchie Ginther Aston Martin P212 which retired in the 7th hour after strongly challenging for the lead at Le Mans.

Opposite, bottom: The 246SP Ferrari driven by Ricardo and Pedro Rodriguez in the 1962 Sebring 12 Hours race before it retired with engine trouble.

1963
Jim Clark wins with maximum points

Jim Clark

The 1.5 litre Formula had produced full starting grids and some close racing and so the C.S.I decided to extend it beyond 1963 to 1966. For 1963 Coventry-Climax produced an improved version of their V8 engine with fuel injection and B.R.M. had a new car designated the P61 which had a 6 speed gearbox and eventually replaced the Championship winning P57. The P61 had a monocoque centre section with space frames front and back. Colin Chapman stayed with his Lotus 25 while Ferrari, like B.R.M, produced a semi-monocoque for its new driver John Surtees. Porsche had withdrawn from racing at the end of 1962. Ken Gregory's British Racing Partnership (B.R.P) raced Lotus–B.R.Ms and a monocoque car of its own design which resembled the Lotus 25. There were two BT7 Brabham-Climax cars available for Jack Brabham and Dan Gurney. Joakim Bonnier was to drive Rob Walker's Cooper-Climax. Bowmaker withdrew its support from Lola but the cars were bought by Reg Parnell and driven by Chris Amon and Maurice Trintignant. A new Italian car called the A.T.S (Automobili Turismo e Sport) would be driven by Phil Hill and Giancarlo Baghetti but without success. Sadly Ricardo Rodriquez had been killed at the end of 1962 during practice for the non Championship Mexican Grand Prix.

THE WORLD CHAMPIONSHIP SERIES

Monaco Grand Prix: May 26

The works teams had no guaranteed places at Monaco in 1963 as only the past winners of the race and World Champions were assured of a place on the grid. The cars were generally little changed from the previous year. Jim Clark's Lotus 25 and the B.R.M. P57s of Graham Hill and Richie Ginther were new cars built to 1962 specifications and with improved engines. John Surtees was driving for Ferrari and Dan Gurney for Brabham. Ken Tyrrell now managed the Cooper team as John Cooper was recovering from a major accident with a twin engined Mini. The B.R.P. team had Lotus 24s with B.R.M. engines and Reg Parnell Racing had two Lola-Climax cars.

Jim Clark was fastest in practice and he had Graham Hill alongside him on the front row. Behind them were John Surtees (Tipo 156 Ferrari) and Ritchie Ginther. Then came Innes Ireland (B.R.P. Lotus-B.R.M.), Dan Gurney (Brabham-Climax), Willy Mairesse (Ferrari), and Bruce McLaren (Cooper-Climax.) Jack Brabham was at the very back of the grid with a borrowed Lotus 25 after experiencing a major engine problem during practice and having no time left to improve his position.

At the start the B.R.Ms of Hill and Ginther led from Clark's Lotus–Climax and John Surtees' Ferrari. Clark squeezed past Ginther on lap 5 and Graham Hill on lap 7. Then Hill was soon past him again and the two were side by side on a number of occasions before

Clark finally overtook Hill on lap 17 and proceeded to open up a useful lead. Dan Gurney (Brabham-Climax) pulled out on lap 26 with a broken crown wheel and pinion and Surtees passed Ginther on lap 28. Surtees got past Hill eventually but then had to surrender his position, dropping back to change to his spare goggles. After this his car suffered a loss of oil pressure. The race appeared to be virtually over when Clark's gearbox jammed, causing his abrupt retirement on lap 79. He was credited with 8th place, 22 laps behind the winner. **So it was Graham Hill's race at a record 72.424 mph.** Ginther (B.R.M.) was second and then came McLaren (Cooper-Climax), Surtees (Ferrari) Maggs (Cooper-Climax), Trevor Taylor (Lotus-Climax) and Joakim Bonnier (Cooper-Climax). The fastest lap of the race was recorded by Surtees' Ferrari at 74.446 mph.

BGA

Aerial view of Ritchie Ginther's B.R.M. at Monaco.

Belgian Grand Prix: June 9

Phil Hill and Giancarlo Baghetti arrived in Spa with the new Italian A.T.S cars and Tony Settember brought the Scirocco-B.R.M. in American colours. The highest placed of the three in practice was Phil Hill in 17th place. Cooper had a more streamlined car for Bruce McLaren who was 5th in practice. B.R.M. and Lotus were both preoccupied with gearbox problems and Trevor Taylor crashed when the rear suspension of his Lotus-Climax failed. Eventually Graham Hill's B.R.M. was fastest and he had Dan Gurney (Brabham-Climax) and Willy Mairesse (Ferrari) with him on the front row of the grid. Innes Ireland was 5th in the B.R.P-B.R.M. and Jim Clark only 6th in his Lotus-Climax after sitting through most of the practice while his gearbox was sorted.

At the start Clark came through from the third row to lead from Graham Hill, and the two left Jack Brabham (Brabham-Climax) well back in third place by the end of the first lap. Mairesse passed Brabham, and McLaren (Cooper-Climax) separated the Brabhams of Jack Brabham and Gurney who were in 4th and 6th places. Then Mairesse lost places and retired on lap 7 with engine trouble. It was now Surtees (Ferrari) that took up the chase after the distant pair, while Brabham dropped back and eventually retired with an electrical fault. After Surtees stopped at his pit for repairs Gurney (Brabham-Climax) and McLaren occupied 3rd and 4th positions. With Clark and Graham Hill in front, the four cars circulated at some distance from each other. Then on lap 18 Graham Hill's new six speed gearbox seized up and his race was run. Heavy rain with thunder and lightning caused a number of spins so that Colin Chapman of Lotus and Tony Rudd of B.R.M. pressed for the race to be stopped. In spite of this the race as allowed to run its course with **Clark the clear winner at 114.100 mph** from McLaren (Cooper-Climax), Gurney (Brabham-Climax), Ginther (B.R.M.) and Bonnier (Cooper-Climax). Settember was classified 8th, five laps in arrears, while the two A.T.S cars which also failed to finish were unclassified. Fastest lap of the race was recorded by Clark at 132.468 mph.

Dutch Grand Prix: June 23

The new semi monocoque P61 B.R.M. was brought to Zandvoort but Graham Hill had problems relating to its suspension and brakes and decided to use his P57, now known as "Old Faithful," for the race. Jim Clark was in pole position with Graham Hill (B.R.M.) and Bruce McLaren (Cooper-Climax) alongside. Jack Brabham (Brabham-Climax) and John Surtees (Ferrari) were 4th and 5th in the second row. The A.T.S cars of Phil Hill and

Ludovico Scarfiotti in the Dino 156 Ferrari before finishing in sixth place in the 1962 Dutch Grand Prix.

Giancarlo Baghetti were 13th and 15th, both drivers no doubt wishing that they were back with Ferrari.

Clark led coming out of the first corner from Graham Hill and McLaren but Jack Brabham moved up to 3rd place when the Cooper's gearbox proved to be difficult. As Clark continued to lead the race Brabham passed Graham Hill, whose engine was running hot, while Gurney (Brabham-Climax) steadily improved his position, having being left behind at the start. On lap 19 Graham Hill was back in second place, having retrieved his position from Brabham, and Brabham now had Surtees in his mirrors. Gurney was delayed at his pit having his exhaust pipe secured and, setting off in 7th place, pressed on again after the leaders undeterred. On lap 55 Brabham spun with a jammed throttle and Graham Hill's B.R.M. had to stop for water four laps later. The B.R.M. rejoined the race at a great pace but its engine gave way on lap 70 having recovered to 3rd place behind Clark and Gurney. **Clark won by a clear lap, having led from start to finish,** at 97.528 mph. Gurney was a magnificent 2nd, Surtees 3rd, Innes Ireland (B.R.P-B.R.M.) 4th, and Richie Ginther 5th. Clark also achieved the fastest lap of the race at 100.100 mph.

Dan Gurney who would take second place at Zandvoort in his Brabham-Climax.

French Grand Prix: June 30

The A.T.S team stayed away from Rheims but Tony Settember was there with the Scirocco-B.R.M. There were three works Lotus 25s for Jim Clark, Trevor Taylor and Peter Arundell, the first with a ZF gearbox and the others with Colotti units. Graham Hill and Richie Ginther had the new semi monocoque P61 and two P57s, and a fourth B.R.M, "Old Faithful", was entered by Cento Sud for Lorenzo Bandini and painted in Italian red. John Surtees' lone Ferrari had new engine air scoops and the Coopers arrived with enlarged radiator cowls. The Parnell team had a Lotus-Climax for Maurice Trintignant, a Lola-Climax for Chris Amon and a Lola-B.R.M. for Masten Gregory. The British Racing Partnership had the B.R.P-B.R.M. for Innes Ireland, and Lotus-B.R.Ms for Jim Hall and Jo Siffert. Clark was fastest in practice, Graham Hill second in the new P61 B.R.M, and Dan Gurney third in his Brabham-Climax. Then came John Surtees and Jack Brabham in one of his own cars. Bandini was last of all with even the Scirocco-B.R.M. ahead of him. Immediately before the race Hill's B.R.M, Phil Hill's Lotus-B.R.M. and Masten Gregory's Lotus-B.R.M. all refused to start and, contrary to the rules, they were allowed to be push started.

At the start Clark quickly established a clear lead with Gurney, Graham Hill, Brabham and Ginther, up from the 5th row, all battling for 2nd place. This tightly bunched set began to unravel as Ginther stopped with a holed radiator, Gurney with a broken gear lever and Surtees with fuel starvation. Out on his own Clark's Lotus was followed at a distance by Brabham (Brabham-Climax), Taylor (Lotus-Climax), McLaren (Cooper-Climax) and Graham Hill (B.R.M.). Next Taylor stopped for a new battery and McLaren slowed with mechanical problems so that the order became Clark, Brabham and Graham Hill. Clark's Lotus was losing power but rain assisted him in holding on to a diminishing lead. Then Brabham stopped for repairs on lap 43 and **at the end it was Clark's Lotus-Climax that chalked up another clear win,** at 125.311 mph, from Tony Maggs (Cooper-Climax), Graham Hill (B.R.M.), who like Phil Hill and Masten Gregory had been penalised by one minute for being push started, Brabham (Brabham-Climax) and Dan Gurney (Brabham-Climax). Bandini finished in 10th place in the red B.R.M, 8 laps behind the winner. Clark also scored the fastest lap at 131.147 mph. Graham Hill in addition had his points for third place deducted because of the outside assistance he had received at the start.

British Grand Prix: July 20

There were eleven Coventry-Climax engined cars at Silverstone for the British Grand Prix and ten cars with B.R.M. engines. B.R.M. had decided to revert to the trusty 1962 P57 cars with the latest engines and 6 speed gearboxes. A third P57 finished in red and driven by Lorenzo Bandini was managed by B.R.M. for Centro-Sud. Jim Clark's V8 Lotus 25 had fuel injection. Graham Hill was 3rd in practice to Clark's Lotus-Climax and Dan Gurney's Brabham-Climax. Jack Brabham completed the front row in one of his own cars. Bandini was 7th fastest in the Centro Sud B.R.M. and the famous racing motor cyclist Mike Hailwood drove a Lola in Reg Parnell's team to 17th place on the starting grid.

Starting Grid

J. Brabham	G. Hill	D. Gurney	J.Clark
Brabham-Climax	B.R.M	Brabham-Climax	Lotus-Climax
1 min 35.0 secs	1 min 34.8 secs	1 min 34.6 secs	1 min 34.4 secs

A. Maggs	B. McLaren	J. Surtees
Cooper-Climax	Cooper-Climax	Ferrari
1 min 36 secs	1 min 35.4 secs	1 min 35.2 secs

I. Ireland	T. Taylor	P.R. Ginther	L. Bandini
B.R.P–B.R.M	Lotus-Climax	B.R.M	B.R.M
1 min 36.8 secs	1 min 36.8 secs	1 min 36 secs	1 min 36 secs

C. Amon	J. Hall	J. Bonnier
Lola-Climax	Lotus-B.R.M	Cooper-Climax
1 min 37.2 secs	1 min 37.0 secs	1 min 36.8 secs

T. Settember	S.M.B. Hailwood	R. Anderson	J. Siffert
Scirocco-B.R.M	Lotus-Climax	Lola-Climax	Lotus-B.R.M
1 min 48.0 secs	1 min 39.8 secs	1 min 39.0 secs	1 min 38.4 secs

C.G. de Beaufort	I. Burgess	I. Raby
Porsche	Scirocco-B.R.M	Gilby-B.R.M
1 min 43.4 secs	1 min 42.6 secs	1 min 42.4 secs

J. Campbell-Jones	M. Gregory
Lola-Climax	Lotus-B.R.M
1 min 48.8 secs	1 min 44.2 secs

Jim Clark made an uncharacteristically poor start and the Brabhams of Jack Brabham and Dan Gurney led Bruce McLaren's Cooper, Graham Hill's B.R.M, and Clark into the first bend. However, Clark carved his way past each one in turn to lead the race and to begin to draw away from the others by lap 5. McLaren was the first to drop away with engine trouble on lap 7. The order then became Clark, Brabham, Gurney, Hill and Surtees. In the laps that followed Gurney overtook Brabham, and Surtees overtook Hill. Gurney was

John Surtees in his Tipo 156 Ferrari at Silverstone during the British Grand Prix.

Jim Clark winning the 1963 British Grand Prix in his Lotus-Climax.

forced to retire with a major engine failure on lap 60 and Clark now led from Hill and John Surtees (Ferrari) while Richie Ginther (B.R.M.) and Joakim Bonnier (Cooper–Climax) disputed fourth place. Then on lap 66 Bonnier stopped with falling oil pressure, settling the argument in Ginther's favour. **Clark had been careful to conserve his remaining fuel over the last laps of the race but still emerged as the clear winner at 107.35 mph.** Surtees came through in 2nd place as the engine of Graham Hill's

Graham Hill's B.R.M. at Silverstone.

B.R.M. cut out, empty of petrol, on the last lap and the Londoner coasted over the line to finish 3rd with Ginther 4th and Bandini's red Centro Sud car 5th. The fastest lap was posted by Surtees at 109.76 mph.

Results

1. J. Clark	Lotus-Climax	2 hr 14 min 09.6 secs
2. J. Surtees	Ferrari	2 hr 14 min 35.4 secs
3. G. Hill	B.R.M	2 hr 14 min 47.2 secs
4. P.R. Ginther	B.R.M.	1 lap
5. L. Bandini	B.R.M.	
6. J. Hall	Lotus-B.R.M	2 laps
7. C. Amon	Lola-Climax	
8. S.M.B. Hailwood	Lotus-Climax	4 laps
9. A. Maggs	Cooper-Climax	
10. C. G. De Beaufort	Porsche	6 laps
11. M. Gregory	Lotus-B.R.M	7 laps
12 R. Anderson	Lola-Climax	
13. J. Campbell-Jones	Lola-Climax	8 laps

Retirements

B. McLaren Cooper-Climax lap 7 engine; T. Settember Scirocco-B.R.M. lap 21 ignition; T. taylor Lotus-Climax lap 24 fuel pump; I. Ireland B.R.P/B.R.M. lap 28 engine; J. Brabham Brabham-Climax lap 28 engine; I. Burgess Scirocco-B.R.M. lap 37 ignition; D. Gurney Brabham-Climax pap 60 engine; I. Raby Gilby-B.R.M. lap 60 gearbox; J. Bonnier Cooper-Climax lap 66 oil pressure; J. Siffert Lotus-B.R.M. lap 67 gearbox.

German Grand Prix: August 4

Jim Clark was fastest in practice for the German Grand Prix at the Nurburgring in his Lotus 25 and John Surtees' Ferrari, with bolt on cast wheels, was 1.1 seconds slower in 2nd place. Beating the works B.R.M. drivers, Lorenzo Bandini was 3rd in the red Centro Sud "Old Faithful". After trying the new P61 B.R.M. Graham settled for a lightweight P57 and was fourth fastest, 2.9 seconds slower than Bandini. On the third row were Bruce McLaren (Cooper-Climax), Richie Ginther (B.R.M.) and Willy Mairesse (Ferrari). Ken Tyrrell was in charge of the Cooper team as John Cooper was still not fully recovered.

Jack Brabham, whose car had a VW Hewland gearbox, had a dead engine at the start and both Bandini and Surtees were slow off the line. It was Clark who led initially followed by Richie Ginther's B.R.M. and Tony Maggs' Cooper. But Clark's engine sounded rough and he was overtaken by Ginther, and Surtees was soon right behind him. Bandini spun and collected Innes Ireland so that both were out on lap 1. Mairesse (Ferrari) crashed on lap 2 after landing heavily at Flugplatz, and sustained serious injuries. Driving with supreme skill Surtees maintained a strong lead over Clark who passed and then stayed ahead of Ginther. Graham Hill retired on lap 3 when the gearbox of his P57 failed, and McLaren crashed on the following lap. Surtees and Clark passed and re passed each other until on lap 7 Clark begin to fall back with a misfire. Maggs (Cooper-Climax) ran in 4th place until he stopped with engine trouble on lap 8. Then Jo Siffert was 4th with his Lotus-B.R.M. until his differential broke. So **Surtees deservedly won at 95.829 mph** by over a minute from Clark and Ginther. A surprised 4th was Gerhard Mitter in an elderly 4 cylinder Porsche. Surtees also made the fastest lap of the race at 96.820 mph.

Italian Grand Prix: September 8

As neither Willy Mairesse nor Trevor Taylor was fully recovered, Lorenzo Bandini drove the second works Ferrari and Mike Spence the second Lotus. The Centro-Sud B.R.M. was driven by Maurice Trintignant. Ferrari had its new semi-monocoque car at Monza which

Innes Ireland's B.R.P-B.R.M. passing Ritchie Ginther's B.R.M. at Monza while being pursued by Lorenzo Bandini's Ferrari. Behind them are Jack Brabham's Brabham–Climax and Tony Magg's Cooper-Climax.

appeared to have much in common with the Lotus 25, but it had not been sufficiently developed to be used in the race. During practice Bob Anderson crashed on the banking and because of this it was decided not to use that section of the course for the race.

There was fierce competition for pole position at Monza and the partisan crowd was ecstatic when John Surtees secured it in his well tried Ferrari. Graham Hill's P61 B.R.M. was next to him on the front row of the grid and behind them were Jim Clark's Lotus-Climax and Richie Ginther's P57 B.R.M. Bandini was 6th alongside Dan Gurney's Brabham-Climax.

Surtees was slowed by wheelspin at the start and the order was Hill, Clark and Surtees. Then Surtees passed Clark and raced side by side with Hill before getting in front. Clark, taking advantage of Surtees's slipstream, also passed Hill and then Surtees tried to gain clear air between himself and his pursuers. Gurney caught up with Hill who began to lose the leading pair and Surtees held on to a slender lead from Clark until lap 17 when the Ferrari engine cried "Enough." Behind Clark, Gurney and Hill came Ginther, Bandini and Innes Ireland. Then, after a gap, came Brabham, McLaren and Bonnier. The crowd groaned when Bandini retired on lap 38 with gearbox trouble. Hill dropped out of contention with a failing clutch and Clark shook off Gurney when the American slowed with fuel starvation to finally stop on lap 63. **It was a further convincing win for Clark** at 127.738 mph from Ginther's B.R.M, McLaren's Cooper and Innes Ireland's B.R.P.-B.R.M. Ireland was forced to surrender 3rd place on the penultimate lap when his engine seized up. Clark also established the fastest lap at 130.054 mph.

United States Grand Prix: October 6

Driving two P57 B.R.Ms Graham Hill and Richie Ginther were 1st and 4th in practice for the United States Grand Prix at Watkins Glen. Jim Clark's Lotus-Climax was 2nd and John Surtees Ferrari 3rd. Lorenzo Bandini was 9th in the second works Ferrari and the Brabhams of Jack Brabham and Dan Gurney were 5th and 6th. Reg Parnell had a Lola-Climax for Masten Gregory and Lotus-B.R.Ms for Roger Ward and Hap Sharp. They were 8th, 17th and 18th. Pedro Rodriguez was 13th fastest in a third works Lotus 25. When the cars rolled forward from the dummy grid Clark's Lotus 25 was found to have a flat battery so, being left behind, had to have a new battery fitted after the pack had left. Graham Hill and Ginther led Surtees and Gurney away on the first lap but Surtees gained on the B.R.Ms and was in the lead by lap 7. Gurney also succeeded in passing the two cars from Bourne. Surtees maintained his lead but Graham Hill regained 2nd place ahead of Gurney, Brabham and Ginther and then challenged Surtees. Gurney retired on lap 43 with fuel starvation while Graham Hill and Surtees passed and re-passed each other until late on in the race when Surtees established a firm lead. At the same time Graham Hill's anti-roll bar became loose and caused his car to understeer. The race appeared to be Surtees' until he was forced to stop with a collapsed piston. Clark had traded places after his late start and in spite of a misfire managed to finish in 3rd place one lap behind the winner. **Graham Hill won at an average speed of 108.920 mph.** Ginther was 2nd, Clark 3rd, Brabham 4th and Bandini 5th. Clark established the fastest lap of the race at 111.141 mph.

Mexican Grand Prix: October 27

Jim Clark (Lotus-Climax) was fastest in practice in Mexico City with John Surtees in the monocoque Ferrari next to him on the grid. Behind were Graham Hill (B.R.M.) and Dan Gurney (Brabham-Climax) and, in the third row, Richie Ginther (B.R.M.) and Bruce McLaren (Cooper-Climax). Lorenzo Bandini was 7th now proudly driving a second and brand new monocoque Ferrari. Trevor Taylor was back in a Lotus-Climax in 12th place. Last of all was Giancarlo Baghetti in the A.T.S. The B.R.M. engines had modified cams and were re-tuned to accommodate the high altitude. The red Centro Sud car was driven by the Mexican driver Moises Solana and Chris Amon was back in Reg Parnell's Lotus-B.R.M. Surtees, whose judgement was good, urgently asked for his car's tyre pressures to be reduced on the starting grid but his request was denied.

At the start it was Clark who led from Surtees and Gurney, while Hill had difficulty in selecting a gear. Gurney was pursued by Bruce McLaren (Cooper-Climax), Ginther and Jack Brabham (Brabham-Climax). Gurney passed Surtees and both Ginther and Brabham passed McLaren. Pedro Rodriguez, driving a Lotus-Climax was gaining places further down the field. Clark continued to extend his lead in his Lotus 25 while Brabham passed Surtees who was disqualified for requiring a push to restart his Ferrari after he had stopped at his pit to have his tyre pressures reduced. Now the order was Clark, Gurney, Brabham, Ginther, McLaren, Hill and Bandini. McLaren retired on lap 30 with engine trouble and Gurney dropped back through the field. **Clark won the race after another tremendous performance,** having led from the start and never been challenged.

John Surtees' Ferrari leading Jack Brabham's Brabham-Climax during the Mexican Grand Prix prior to being disqualified for receiving assistance.

Brabham was 2nd, Graham Hill 3rd, Bonnier 4th, and Gurney 5th. Clark's average speed was 93.300 mph and he established the fastest lap of the race at 94.705 mph.

South African Grand Prix: December 28

Ferrari arrived in East London with two monocoques and a spare space framed car for John Surtees and Lorenzo Bandini. Jim Clark, who already had the World Championship securely in his grasp, was fastest in practice with his Lotus-Climax and he, with the Brabhams of Jack Brabham and Dan Gurney, formed the front row of the grid. The Ferraris of Surtees and Bandini occupied the second row, and Graham Hill (B.R.M.), Richie Ginther (B.R.M.) and Trevor Taylor (Lotus-Climax) the third. Unusual additions to the grid were two L.D.S-Alfa Romeos (built by Louis Douglas Serrurier) and an Alfa Special.

Brabham fractionally anticipated the start but he was overtaken by both Clark and Surtees during the course of the first lap. Then, after Brabham, came Taylor, Bandini, Bruce McLaren (Cooper-Climax), Ginther and Hill. Taylor lost his 4th position to Gurney, and Surtees' Ferrari was overtaken by both Brabham and Gurney on lap 6. Gurney then overtook Brabham who dropped back, while Clark steadily increased his lead. On lap 15 Graham Hill passed Brabham, and Ginther passed both Bruce McLaren and Brabham. Surtees retired on lap 44 with a blown engine and, on the same lap, Ginther retired with a broken drive shaft. Taylor lost time with gear selector difficulties and Brabham, having spun on lap 71, retired with a split fuel tank. In the end **Clark's Lotus-Climax won by over a minute** from Dan Gurney (Brabham-Climax), Graham Hill (B.R.M.) Bruce McLaren (Cooper-Climax) and Lorenzo Bandini (Ferrari). Dan Gurney registered the fastest lap of the race at 98.407 mph.

Dan Gurney's Brabham-Climax passing John Surtees' Ferrari to finish second in the South African Grand Prix.

The World Championship

Jim Clark won the World Championship with seven wins, a record that wouldn't be beaten until 1988 when Ayrton Senna managed eight wins.

Clark had 54 points, Graham Hill and Richie Ginther each had 29, John Surtees 22, Dan Gurney 19, Bruce McLaren 17 and Jack Brabham 14.

The Constructors' World Championship was won by Lotus–Climax with 54 points. B.R.M. was second with 36, Brabham-Climax third with 28. Then came Ferrari with 26, Cooper-Climax with 25, B.R.P–B.R.M. with 6, Porsche with 5 and Lotus-B.R.M. with 4.

The International Trophy Race at Silverstone

Innes Ireland (Lotus-B.R.M.) was fastest in practice at Silverstone while Graham Hill's B.R.M. was 2nd and Trevor Taylor's Lotus–Climax 3rd, but in the race it was Jim Clark's

Lorenzo Bandini driving "Old Faithful" in the Italian colours of Centro Sud during the 1963 International Trophy Race at Silverstone, before being disqualified for being push started after a pit stop.

Lotus-Climax that came through to win the Trophy from Bruce McLaren's Cooper-Climax and Trevor Taylor's Lotus-Climax. Lorenzo Bandini's red B.R.M. was disqualified for being push started after a pit stop and Graham Hill's works B.R.M. retired with electrical problems. Willy Mairesse crashed out of the race in his lone Ferrari. Two Scirocco-B.R.Ms and an A.T.S failed to arrive.

The Gold Cup race at Oulton Park

Jim Clark (Lotus-Climax) was in pole position for the Gold Cup Race with Graham Hill (B.R.M.) 2nd in practice and Trevor Taylor (Lotus-Climax) 3rd. The race was won by Clark from Ritchie Ginther (B.R.M.) and Graham Hill. Jack Brabham (Cooper-Climax) was 4th and Tony Maggs (Cooper-Climax) 5th. Ian Burgess qualified in 18th place in a Scirocco-B.R.M. and finished the race in 8th position.

Graham Hill (B.R.M.) lapping Ian Burgess (Scirocco-B.R.M.) during the 1963 Gold Cup Race at Oulton Park.

Monte Carlo Rally

In the course of the exceptionally cold winter of 1962/1963 the 296 competitors in the Monte Carlo Rally faced the most hazardous conditions with some of the roads blocked with snow and ice. Nevertheless 27 cars completed the road section without penalty points. The Rally would have been won by Ljungfeldt and Haggborn in an American Ford Falcon Futura had they not lost half an hour with clutch failure. The actual winner was Eric Carlsson's Saab. The Team Prize went to Citroen with Biachi, Neyret and Verrier finishing 2nd, 4th and 5th. The highest placed British entry was a Morris Mini Cooper driven by Hopkirk and Scott into 6th place.

Targa Florio

The issue once again lay between Ferrari and Porsche and, as usual, there were no neutrals within the crowd that was scattered around the 44 mile route. There were 8 cylinder 2 litre Porsches for Bonnier/Abate and Maglioli/Baghetti, and 3 litre V12 250P Ferraris for Surtees/Parkes and Vaccarella/Mairesse. Bandini/Scarfiotti had a 2 litre V6 Ferrari and there were also Ferrari GTOs and Porsche Carreras. In addition to the German and Italian cars there was a privately entered Aston Martin DB4 and an E Type Jaguar.

On the first lap Bonnier led from Maglioli, and the two Porsches were followed by the Ferraris of Scarfiotti, Parkes and Bandini. By the second lap a number of cars were missing and others showed distinct signs of having unintentionally left the road. The order became Parkes, Bonnier, Bandini, Maglioli, Bulgari (Ferrari GTO 3 litre). On lap five Surtees, having taken over from Parkes, damaged his fuel tank during an unscheduled excursion, and so retired, while Abate, now driving in place of Bonnier led in the Porsche. Behind Bonnier came Scarfiotti/Bandini (Ferrari), and Maglioli/Baghetti (Porsche). Baghetti then joined the retirements when he lost most of his gears and Bonnier, out in front, was also experiencing some difficulties in that department. He held on until the end winning the 47th Targo Florio from the Bandini/Scarfiotti Ferrari and the Linge/Barth 4 cylinder 2 litre Porsche.

Le Mans

Aston Martin came with a Prototype 215 with a 4 litre engine and two DB4 GT Coupes; there were three works 250P Ferraris and a front engined 4.1 litre car entered by N.A.R.T. Briggs Cunningham had three lightweight E Type Jaguars and two AC Cobras with 4.7 litre Ford engines.

Phil Hill led for the first lap with the Prototype Aston Martin and Graham Hill was held at the line to be started last of all in the Rover B.R.M. turbine car. The rear axle broke on the Aston Martin in the second hour and, apart from a brief spell when Simon's Maserati was in front, the race was dominated by the Ferraris. Surtees led, followed by Parkes while Graham

The 250P Ferrari of Ludovico Scarfiotti and Lorenzo Bandini winning the 1963 Le Mans 24 Hour race.

Graham Hill silently and effectively circulating at Le Mans in the Rover-B.R.M.

Hill surprised everyone as he steadily passed the back markers in the turbine car. The Parkes/Maglioli Ferrari was delayed with ignition trouble but, half way through the race, Ferraris occupied the first six places and this remained the case until the end. Remarkably, the Rover B.R.M. was up to 8th place by the twenty-second hour. It was another Ferrari win with the Scarfiotti/Bandini car covering 2834.51 miles at 118.11 mph.

The Aston Martin DB4 GT of McLaren/Ireland retired in the sixth hour and that of Schlesser/Kimberley retired in the eleventh hour after running in third place at one stage. The Aston Martin DB4 GT Zagato of Franc/Kerguen retired in the seventh hour . An Austin-Healey Sprite driven by Whitmore/Olthoff retired in the ninth hour. Of Briggs Cunningham's E Type Jaguars, the one driven by Richards/Grossmann finished in 9th place and won the 4 litre class, while those of Hansgen/Pabst and Salvadori/Cunningham retired in the first and sixth hours. A Lister-Jaguar driven by Sargent/Lumsden retired in the third hour after becoming beached in the sand; an MGB driven by Hopkirk/Hutcheson finished 12th and was 2nd in the 2 litre class. Of two Lotus Elites, one driven by Wagstaff/Fergusson was placed 10th, winning the class for GT cars of less than 2 litres, and the other, driven by Gardner/Coundley retired in the sixteenth hour. .

The Tourist Trophy Race at Goodwood

Graham Hill was fastest in practice in his Ferrari 250 GTO and Mike Parkes was 2nd in an identical car from Marenello. After them came the Aston Martin DP 214s of Innes Ireland and Bruce McLaren. Roy Salvadori drove a lightweight E Type Jaguar and Roger Penske yet another Ferrari 250 GTO.

Hill led from Ireland and Parkes until Ireland made contact with Hill in attempting to pass him. Both were able to continue but Ireland had to stop for new tyres having flat spotted his first set. This put Hill back in front while behind him Parkes and Ireland both spun. Hill held his lead until the end with Parkes 2nd, Savadori (E Type Jaguar) 3rd, Jack Sears (E Type Jaguar) 4th, David Piper (Ferrari 250 GTO) 5th and Ireland's Aston Martin 7th.

Graham Hill standing at the ready beside his 250 GTO Ferrari to win the 1963 Tourist Trophy Race at Goodwood.

1964

John Surtees supreme on four wheels too

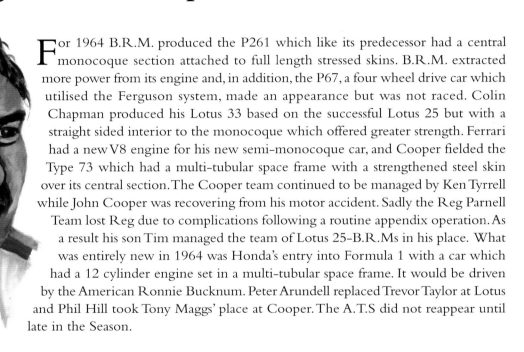

John Surtees.

For 1964 B.R.M. produced the P261 which like its predecessor had a central monocoque section attached to full length stressed skins. B.R.M. extracted more power from its engine and, in addition, the P67, a four wheel drive car which utilised the Ferguson system, made an appearance but was not raced. Colin Chapman produced his Lotus 33 based on the successful Lotus 25 but with a straight sided interior to the monocoque which offered greater strength. Ferrari had a new V8 engine for his new semi-monocoque car, and Cooper fielded the Type 73 which had a multi-tubular space frame with a strengthened steel skin over its central section. The Cooper team continued to be managed by Ken Tyrrell while John Cooper was recovering from his motor accident. Sadly the Reg Parnell Team lost Reg due to complications following a routine appendix operation. As a result his son Tim managed the team of Lotus 25-B.R.Ms in his place. What was entirely new in 1964 was Honda's entry into Formula 1 with a car which had a 12 cylinder engine set in a multi-tubular space frame. It would be driven by the American Ronnie Bucknum. Peter Arundell replaced Trevor Taylor at Lotus and Phil Hill took Tony Maggs' place at Cooper. The A.T.S did not reappear until late in the Season.

The World Championship Series

Monaco Grand Prix: May 10

Ferrari brought their latest semi-monocoque Tipo 158 V8 car to Monaco for John Surtees and regrettably the distinctive shark nose had been discarded. Both B.R.M. and Cooper had their 1964 cars on hand for this first race of the Season. Colin Chapman had to rely upon his championship winning Lotus 25Bs as the new Lotus 33 had been crashed by Jim Clark before the Season began. Innes Ireland crashed his B.R.P-B.R.M. during practice for the race and so was a non starter. It was Jim Clark who won pole position in his Lotus-Climax and Jack Brabham was next to him at the front of the grid in his Brabham-Climax. Then came Graham Hill's B.R.M. and John Surtees' Ferrari, so there were four different makes represented by the first four cars. Maurice Trintignant drove the "Old Faithful" B.R.M, now in blue livery, and he was 13th in practice.

Clark stormed into the lead and held on to it in spite of clouting with some force the straw bales at the chicane on the first lap. He was followed by Brabham, Graham Hill, Dan Gurney (Brabham-Climax), Surtees, and Ritchie Ginther (B.R.M.). Gurney overtook Hill on lap 12 and Ginther overtook Surtees, but Clark increased his lead over them all. Surtees stopped at his pit with trouble relating to his gearbox and retired on lap 15. Trevor Taylor (B.R.P-B.R.M.) retired with a fuel leak while Clark remained out in front, his pace not slackened by an anti-roll bar which flapped after his incident at the chicane. He

Jim Clark leading the 1964 Monaco Grand Prix in his Lotus-Climax.

stopped on lap 37 to have the bar removed and rejoined the race in third place behind Gurney and Hill. On lap 53 Graham Hill passed Gurney to lead the race, breaking the lap record in the process, and Clark took up second position when Gurney retired with gearbox trouble on lap 62 but his engine was running low on oil and it seized on his penultimate lap. So **Graham Hill's B.R.M. won at 72.644 mph** from Richie Ginther (B.R.M.) and Peter Arundell (Lotus-Climax), Clark being classified 4th. Hill also established the fastest lap of the race at 74.922 mph, a new record.

Dutch Grand Prix: May 24

Ferrari arrived with two V8 cars and a spare V6 for John Surtees and Lorenzo Bandini. The B.R.Ms of Graham Hill and Ritcher Ginther were unchanged following Monaco whereas the Lotus 25C and 25D of Jim Clark and Peter Arundell had been provided with strengthened anti roll bars. The Centro Sud B.R.Ms of Tony Maggs and Giancarlo Baghetti were 1963 cars and Maggs overturned his during practice. Joakim Bonnier drove Rob Walker's new Brabham-B.R.M.

The front row of the grid consisted of Dan Gurney (Brabham-Climax), Jim Clark (Lotus-Climax) and Graham Hill (B.R.M.). Then came John Surtees (Ferrari) and Bruce McLaren (Cooper-Climax). The Ferraris of Surtees and Bandini were 4th and 10th in the line up.

At the start there was much wheel-spin on the front row but Clark led Graham Hill, Gurney, Arundell, Surtees and Phil Hill (Cooper-Climax) on the first lap. Surtees overtook Arundell on lap 3 and Gurney on lap 10. On lap 24 Gurney retired with a broken steering wheel as the team lacked a replacement. Both works B.R.Ms were slowed with fuel feed problems and Lorenzo Bandini (Ferrari) retired on lap 26 with fuel injection difficulties. Graham Hill stopped at his pits for some tweaking in the engine department and resumed with his car rejuvenated. He recovered to 4th place by the end of the race. **It was an emphatic win for Clark after an untroubled race at 98.017 mph,** Surtees (Ferrari) was second, 54 seconds behind, and Peter Arundell (Lotus-Climax) third. Clark also set the fastest lap of the race at 101.071 mph.

Belgian Grand Prix: June 14

Jim Clark had to choose between the new Lotus 33 and the older Lotus 25 and he decided upon the earlier car when he found that he couldn't improve upon 6th place with the new model. The B.R.Ms had 6 speed gearboxes and modified fuel systems. The front row of the grid was composed of Dan Gurney (Brabham-Climax), Graham Hill (B.R.M.) and Jack Brabham (Brabham-Climax). Immediately behind them were Peter Arundell (Lotus-Climax), John Surtees (Ferrari) and Jim Clark.

It was Arundell who was quickest off the line but he was soon overtaken by Gurney, Surtees, Clark and Graham Hill. Next time round Surtees was in front but his race ended on lap 4 with engine trouble. Behind Gurney's Brabham, Graham Hill and Clark battled for second place, often side by side and taking turns to go in front. Then they became separated by Bruce McLaren for a time before Clark overtook the Cooper-Climax. Arundell dropped right back when his Lotus overheated and Graham Hill made his second spot secure, being sandwiched by Gurney and Clark. Gurney relinquished his lead when he stopped for fuel but, finding none in his pit, he returned to the fray again. Meanwhile Graham Hill, having inherited the lead, was followed by McLaren's Cooper-Climax which had passed Clark on lap 28. Gurney charged after McLaren but his engine was now starved of fuel and he was forced to stop for good on lap 30. Graham Hill was then next to stop as his tank also ran dry. It only remained for McLaren to be overtaken by **Clark who became the surprise winner of the race at 132.792 mph.** McLaren coasted across the line to finish in 2rd place with an empty tank! Jack Brabham (Brabham-Climax) was 3rd, Ritchie Ginther (B.R.M.) 4th, Graham Hill classified 5th, and Dan Gurney 6th. The fastest lap went to Dan Gurney at 137.613 mph.

French Grand Prix: June 28

There were three P261 B.R.Ms for Graham Hill and Ritchie Ginther at Rouen and all of them spent much of the practice sessions in the pits. Once more Jim Clark was able to choose between a Lotus 33 and a Lotus 25 and he again close the earlier model.

Jim Clark leading the French Grand Prix in his Lotus 25 before a broken piston ended his race.

Dan Gurney's Brabham-Climax overtaking Chris Amon's Lotus-B.R.M. to win the French Grand Prix.

Clark was fastest in practice in his Lotus-Climax, Dan Gurney, 2nd in his Brabham-Climax and John Surtees 3rd in his Ferrari. Then came Peter Arundell (Lotus-Climax) and Jack Brabham (Brabham-Climax). Graham Hill was 6th, Bandini (Ferrari) 8th Ginther 10th and Phil Hill 10th in a Cooper-Climax.

Clark's Lotus 25 was leaking oil on the dummy grid and had to be replaced at the last minute by the spare car. Undaunted by this, Clark established an immediate lead followed by Gurney and Surtees while Bruce McLaren spun and lost valuable time. Surtees stopped for minor repairs and it was Brabham who followed Clark after a gap. Graham Hill became another spinner. Clark extended his lead while Graham Hill first passed Phil Hill and then Peter Arundell. Then, on lap 30, Clark stopped at his pit and, after resuming the race, stopped finally after two more laps with a broken piston. While Gurney was out in front, Innes Ireland slid off the course in his B.R.P-B.R.M. losing a wheel but he emerged unhurt from the incident. Graham Hill, in 3rd place, was closing on the two Brabhams in front of him and he fought long and hard with Jack Brabham for 2nd place. **The race ending with Dan Gurney chalking up Brabham's first win in a World Championship race.** Graham Hill managed to pass Jack Brabham thus denying his team a 1 – 2 victory. Gurney's winning speed was 108.766 mph and the fastest lap was made by Jack Brabham at 111.370 mph.

British Grand Prix: July 11

The British Grand Prix was organised by the R.A.C and held at Brands Hatch for the first time. Dan Gurney won a 100 bottles of champagne for establishing the fastest lap in the first session of practice in his Brabham-Climax. Trevor Taylor crashed his B.R.P-B.R.M. and jumped into a Lotus-B.R.M. instead. The experimental four wheel drive B.R.M. was driven by Richard Attwood to good effect but it didn't appear on Sunday for the race.

Starting Grid

D. Gurney	G. Hill	J. Clark
Brabham-Climax	B.R.M	Lotus-Climax
1 min 38.4 secs	1 min 38.3 secs	1 min 38.1 secs

J. Surtees	J. Brabham
Ferrari	Brabham-Climax
1 min 38.7 secs	1 min 38. 5 secs

L. Bandini	R. Anderson	B. McLaren
Ferrari	Brabham-Climax	Cooper-Climax
1 min 40.2 secs	1 min 39.8 secs	1 min 39.6 secs

I. Ireland	J. Bonnier
B.R.P-B.R.M	Brabham-B.R.M
1 min 40.8 secs	1 min 40.2 secs

M. Spence	S.M.B. Hailwood	C. Amon
Lotus-Climax	Lotus-B.R.M	Lotus-B.R.M
1 min 41.4 secs	1 min 41.4 secs	1 min 41.2 secs

P. Hill	P.R. Ginther
Cooper-Climax	B.R.M
1 min 42.6 secs	1 min 41.6 secs

T. Taylor	I. Raby	J. Siffert
Lotus-B.R.M	Brabham-B.R.M	Brabham-B.R.M
1 min 42.8 secs	1 min 42.8 secs	1 min 42.8 secs

J. Taylor	F. Gardner
Cooper-Ford	Brabham-Ford
1 min 43.2 secs	1 min 43.0 secs

A. Maggs	P. Revson	G. Baghetti
B.R.M	Lotus-B.R.M	B.R.M
1 min 45.0 secs	1 min 43.4 secs	1 min 43.4 secs

As was the form in 1964, all the cars lined up on a dummy grid after the warm up lap before creeping forward to their starting positions. Chris Amon's clutch failed at the start, causing Jo Siffert to run into Frank Gardner, but everyone else got away smoothly and on the first lap Jim Clark (Lotus-Climax) led Dan Gurney (Brabham-Climax), Graham Hill (B.R.M.), Lorenzo Bandini (Ferrari) and Phil Hill (Cooper-Climax). Gurney lost a lot of time at his pit with ignition trouble and Bruce McLaren (Cooper-Climax) dropped out with a gearbox failure. The race developed into an exciting dual between Clark and Graham Hill with John Surtees (Ferrari) managing to keep a watchful eye on them from behind. Lorenzo Bandini passed Jack Brabham (Brabham-Climax) to follow in the wake of his team mate when Brabham briefly pitted. Clark eventually managed to disengage himself from Graham Hill in the course of lapping back markers so that he was able to ease off towards the end. **Clark won at a speed of 94.140 mph** from Hill, Surtees and Brabham who had regained his position from Bandini.

Clark was also responsible for the fastest lap of the race at 96.560 mph.

Jim Clark (Lotus-Climax) and Graham Hill (B.R.M.) in the order in which they finished the British Grand Prix at Brands Hatch.

Results

1. J. Clark	Lotus-Climax	2 hr 15 min 07.0 secs
2. G. Hill	B.R.M	2 hr 15 min 09.8 secs
3. J. Surtees	Ferrari	2 hr 16 min 27.6 secs
4. J. Brabham	Brabham-Climax	l lap
5. L. Bandini	Ferrari	2 laps
6. P. Hill	Cooper-Climax	
7. R. Anderson	Brabham-Climax	
8. P.R. Ginther	B.R.M	3 laps
9. M. Spence	Lotus-Climax	
10. I. Ireland	B.R.P-B.R.M.	
11. J. Siffert	Brabham-B.R.M	4 laps
12. G. Baghetti	Ferrari	
13. D. Gurney	Brabham-Climax	5 laps
14. J. Taylor	Cooper-Ford	24 laps

Retirements

F. Gardner Brabham-Ford lap 1 accident, B. McLaren Cooper-Climax lap 7 gearbox, C. Amon Lotus-B.R.M. lap 10 clutch, M.B. Hailwood Lotus-B.R.M. lap 17 fractured oil pipe, T. Taylor Lotus-B.R.M. lap 23 sick driver, A. Maggs B.R.M. lap 38 gearbox, I. Raby Brabham-B.R.M. lap 38 rear hub, P. Revson Lotus-B.R.M. lap 44 engine, J. Bonnier Brabham-B.R.M. lap 47 fractured brake pipe.

German Grand Prix: August 2

Ronnie Bucknum arrived with the new V12 Honda at the Nurburgring but its engine failed early on the first practice session and had to be replaced by another. In consequence Bucknum wasn't able to complete the minimum of 5 practice laps and had to start at the

John Surtees Ferrari winning the German Grand Prix after being fastest in practice.

back of the grid. Tim Parnell had two Lotus 25-B.R.Ms for Mike Hailwood and Chris Amon. John Surtees (V8 Ferrari) was fastest and he shared the front row with Jim Clark (Lotus-Climax) Dan Gurney (Brabham-Climax) and Lorenzo Bandini (V6 Ferrari). Graham Hill (B.R.M.) was 5th, Jack Brabham (Brabham-Climax) 6th, and Bruce McLaren (Cooper-Climax) 7th. B.R.M. suffered two blown engines during the course of practice and Richie Ginther was 11th and on the third row. The 4 wheel drive P67 B.R.M. was present but not used in the race. Sadly Carel Godwin de Beaufort crashed in his old Formula 2 Porsche and died of his injuries the next day in hospital.

At the start of the race Bandini established an initial lead but soon the order became Clark followed by Gurney, Surtees and Graham Hill. Surtees got past Clark, and Gurney followed suit on lap 4. Surtees and Gurney then swopped places for the lead until Gurney dropped back with his engine running too hot. Clark dropped out altogether with engine trouble on lap 8. Surtees' Ferrari was well out in front with Graham Hill's B.R.M. sounding rough ahead of Brabham, Bandini, and Gurney. Then Brabham stopped with a broken crown-wheel and pinion letting Bandini up into third place. **So the race was won by John Surtees (Ferrari) at a speed of 96.579 mph**, from Graham Hill (B.R.M.), Lorenzo Bandini (Ferrari) Jo Siffert (Brabham-B.R.M.) and the three B.R.Ms of Maurice Trintignant, Tony Maggs and Richie Ginther. Surtees also set the fastest lap of the race at 98.313 mph.

Austrian Grand Prix: August 23

Austria hosted a World Championship race for the first time on the rough concrete surface of an airfield circuit at Zeltweg which proved to be excessively hard on the cars. A number of them suffered during practice but Graham Hill made the fastest time in his B.R.M, and next to him were John Surtees (Ferrari), Jim Clark (Lotus-Climax) and Dan Gurney (Brabham-Climax). Jochen Rindt, who had previously competed in Formula 2, was 13th in a Rob Walker's Brabham-B.R.M.

Clark was left at the start having problems with his gears, and Graham Hill was delayed with wheel-spin. Jack Brabham's BT11 returned to its pit with fuel starvation and it was Gurney and Surtees who streaked ahead followed by Lorenzo Bandini's V6 Ferrari. Clark soon set after Ritchie Ginther (B.R.M.), Joakim Bonnier (Brabham-Climax) and Bruce McLaren (Cooper-Climax), all of whom were disputing 4th place, while in front Surtees

Giancarlo Baghetti driving the Centro Sud B.R.M. to seventh place in the Austrian Grand Prix after being only fifteenth in practice.

overtook Gurney to lead the race. Graham Hill's drive was over on lap 6 with a sheered distributor and then Surtees pulled out on lap 9 with a broken rear suspension. Gurney found himself to have a clear lead from Bandini but when Clark passed Bandini he set off after the Brabham-Climax. On lap 40 Clark's charge was stopped with a broken drive shaft and eight laps after this Gurney's Brabham succumbed to suspension failure. Now it was Bandini's Ferrari which led from Ginther's B.R.M. and Bonnier's Brabham-Climax. On lap 59 the steering failed on Phil Hill's Cooper-Climax causing it to hit some straw bales which immediately caught fire. Fortunately he was able to escape unharmed. **So Bandini (Ferrari) won at 99.202 mph** from Ginther (B.R.M.) and Bob Anderson (Brabham-Climax). Gurney set the fastest lap of the race at 101.570 mph. Jochen Rindt had retired on lap 59 with a steering failure and only nine of the fourteen starters had survived the course.

Italian Grand Prix: September 6

It had been decided not to use the banked section of the Monza course for the 1964 Italian Grand Prix. Enzo Ferrari came well armed with a new car with a Flat 12 engine, together with two V6s and a V8 semi-monocoques. John Surtees chose a V8 model and he was fastest in practice, followed by Dan Gurney's Brabham-Climax and Graham Hill's P261 B.R.M. Jim Clark's Lotus 25 was next and alongside Bruce McLaren's Cooper-Climax on the second row of the grid. Lorenzo Bandini was 7th on the grid in a V6 Ferrari, after spending much of the practice period driving the new Flat 12 model. Ludovico Scarfiotti drove a second V6 Ferrari and he was in 16th place. Mario Cabral was 19th in the A.T.S which was now being prepared by Alf Francis. Ronnie Bucknum managed 10th place in the V12 Honda.

Graham Hill's clutch seized at the start but all the other drivers somehow managed to avoid him and it was Bruce McLaren (Cooper-Climax) who led from Gurney and Surtees. Soon McLaren was relegated to third place and Surtees overtook Gurney to lead the race. Clark was in close attendance and the four circulated as one. Bucknum's Honda showed a promising turn of speed in the early stages of the race but retired on lap 13 with ineffective brakes. It was a case of constantly changing places at the front but at last Surtees and Gurney became detached from McLaren while a more distant 4th place was being hotly contested by no less than eight drivers! As the race continued the first four cars of

John Surtees (Ferrari) and
Dan Gurney (Brabham-Climax)
battling for the lead at Monza
before the outcome was
settled in Surtees' favour.

Surtees, Gurney, McLaren and Clark were inches from each other again but then Clark retired on lap 28 with a blown engine and Gurney first pitted and then dropped further back through the field with electrical problems. **Surtees' Ferrari won the race for the exultant tifosi at 127.775 mph** and by one minute from McLaren while Bandini managed to pip Ginther's B.R.M. for 3rd place. Surtees also established the fastest lap of the race at 130.186 mph. It was a good day for the Commendatore.

United States Grand Prix: October 4

The Ferraris arrived at Watkins Glen disguised in the blue and white colours of the North American Racing Team after a dispute between Enzo Ferrari and both the F.I.A and the Italian Automobile Club. Nevertheless Ferrari was determined to repeat his recent success and John Surtees was on the front row of the grid in a V8 Ferrari alongside Jim Clark who had put his Lotus-Climax in pole position. Dan Gurney's Brabham-Climax was 3rd and Graham Hill's B.R.M. 4th. It was sad to see the great Phil Hill at the very back with his Cooper-Climax. Lorenzo Bandini had both the Flat 12 and the V6 cars at his disposal but again chose the well tried V6 which he drove to 8th place on the grid. Ritchie Ginther was only 13th in the second B.R.M.

It was Clark who led initially but he was soon passed by Surtees, and also Mike Spence (Lotus-Climax) up from the third row. At the end of the first lap the order was Surtees, Spence, Clark, Graham Hill and Jack Brabham. Hill's B.R.M. improved to 2nd place behind Surtees but then Clark came through to lead the field. Brabham dropped out from 6th place with engine trouble, and Bruce McLaren (Cooper-Climax) stopped for plugs. So the order behind the leading trio was Bandini, Bonnier (Brabham-Climax) and Siffert. Then Clark had to surrender a substantial lead with fuel feed problems and, after stopping, was asked to take over Spence's car. The B.R.M. now led the race unopposed and at the finish **Graham Hill won at 111.100 mph, a clear lap ahead of Surtees** in 2nd place. Jo Siffert was 3rd in his Brabham-B.R.M. The fastest lap of the race went to Clark at 113.893 mph who finished in 7th place in the Spence car.

Mexican Grand Prix: October 25

The Ferraris were still finished in N.A.R.T colours in Mexico City where the World Championship remained very open with Graham Hill just 5 points ahead of John Surtees. Either of these or Jim Clark could win the title. It was Clark who was fastest in practice

B G Apps

John Surtees' blue and white Ferrari leading Mike Spence's Lotus-Climax to win the 1964 Mexican Grand Prix.

with the new Lotus 33 and Dan Gurney second with his Brabham-Climax. Then came Lorenzo Bandini in the Flat 12 Ferrari and John Surtees (V8 Ferrari) Mike Spence (Lotus-Climax) and Graham Hill (B.R.M.). Pedro Rodriguez had a V6 Ferrari in 9th place and Ritchie Ginther's B.R.M. was 11th.

Clark assumed an immediate lead at the start while Graham Hill was delayed when the elastic strap of his goggles annoyingly snapped. Surtees was slow away with a misfiring engine. Behind Clark came Gurney, Bandini, Spence, Bonnier (Brabham-Climax), Jack Brabham (Brabham-Climax), Pedro Rodriguez (Ferrari), Bruce McLaren (Cooper-Climax), Ritchie Ginther (B.R.M.), Graham Hill (B.R.M.), Jo Siffert (Brabham-B.R.M.), Phil Hill (Cooper-Climax), Surtees (V8 Ferrari), Chris Amon (Lotus-B.R.M.), Innes Ireland (B.R.P-B.R.M.), Mario Solana (Lotus-Climax), Trevor Taylor (B.R.P.-B.R.M.), Mike Hailwood (Lotus-B.R.M.) and Hal Sharp (Brabham-B.R.M.). Both Graham Hill and John Surtees began to forge their way up the field from lowly positions, the B.R.M. driver finding himself in 3rd place by the 12th lap with only Clark and Gurney ahead of him. Then Bandini, having been glued to the rear of Hill's car for several laps, touched and caused both to spin, and this resulted in Hill having to stop for some rapid attention to his buckled exhaust pipes. Having recovered from his spin, Bandini, in the Flat 12 Ferrari was able to overtake the V8 car of Surtees, but Graham Hill's hopes for a further World Championship were dashed. It seemed that the 1964 World Championship would belong to Clark but his Lotus-Climax slowed and stopped with a seized engine caused by a fractured oil pipe. Gurney's Brabham now led and Bandini slowed to allow Surtees to pass him and to take the World Championship by means of his 2nd place. **Dan Gurney won at an average speed was 93.321 mph** and the fastest lap of the race was recorded by Clark at 94.489 mph.

The World Championship

John Surtees won the World Championship with 40 points, Graham Hill was 2nd with 39, Jim Clark was 3rd with 32, Lorenzo Bandini and Richie Ginther were jointly 4th with 23, Dan Gurney was 6th with 19, Bruce McLaren 7th with 13, and Peter Arundell jointly 8th with Jack Brabham 11.

The Constructors' World Championship was won by Ferrari with 45 points. B.R.M. was 2nd with 42, Lotus-Climax 3rd with 37, Brabham-Climax 4th with 30, Cooper-Climax 5th with 16, Brabham-B.R.M. 6th with 7, B.R.P-B.R.M. 7th with 5 and Lotus–B.R.M. 9th with 3.

Monte Carlo Rally

Following the success of the American Ford Falcon Sprints in 1963, a Falcon was confidently expected to win the Monte Carlo Rally in 1964. There were eight of them in all, four of which started from Oslo and four from Paris. Two of the Paris starters were those of Graham Hill and Peter Harper. Alex Issigonis was quietly confident that his BMC

Paddy Hopkirk and Henry Liddon winning the 1964 Monte Carlo Rally in their Mini Cooper S.

Bo Ljungfeldt's Ford Falcon putting up the fastest time in the special stages and coming second overall in the Monte Carlo Rally.

Mini Coopers would spoil the Falcon's party and Paddy Hopkirk's Mini Cooper S was one of the Minsk starters, together with Raymond Baxter (Mini) Sydney Allard (Ford Cortina), and some Russian Volgas and Moskoviches. Peter Dimmock started from Monte Carlo in the B.B.C car and other entrants began their Rally from Athens, Frankfurt, Glasgow and Lisbon. They all only encountered a moderate amount of snow, ice and other forms of inclement weather, but Sidney Allard crashed in Czechoslovakia, and Vic Elford collided with a French car near Rheims. There were divided opinions regarding the use of studded tyres which were excellent on snow and ice but a hindrance in clear and dry conditions. The main emphasis of the Rally centred on the special high speed "tests" and it was the Mini Cooper S of Paddy Hopkirk and Henry Liddon which emerged the outright winner from B. L. Jungfeldt and F. Sager (Ford Falcon) and E. Carlsson and G Palm (Saab Sport.) The Team Prize went to the works Minis of Hopkirk, Makinen and Aaltonen. The Coupe des Dames was won by Pat Moss and U. Wirth.

Targa Florio

With no works Ferraris entered for the Targa Florio, Caroll Shelby, the winner of Le Mans in 1959 in an Aston Martin, brought four AC Cobras with V8 Ford engines to Sicily. Porsche was there with 8 cylinder Prototypes and 904 Carreras for the GT category. Paddy Hopkirk had a works Austin Healey Sprite, Jones and Radcliffe a BMC Mini and there were Alpines and Abarth-Simcas in addition to privately entered Ferraris.

Bonnier established an early lead with his 8 cylinder Porsche while Gurney and Phil Hill lay third and fourth in Cobras. The leading Porsche, now driven by Maglioli, dropped back after stopping for repairs and the leader then was Bulgari in a Porsche 904. His race ended with a broken chassis frame, after coming into contact with something solid, and then it was the turn of a GTO Ferrari driven by Facetti to lead, until his rear axle broke. The race was now led by Colin Davis' Porsche 904 and he set up the fastest lap of the race on lap 7. Baron Pucci took over from him for the last two laps to bring the car across the finishing line in first place. 2nd was Innge/Balzarini (Porsche 904 GTS), 3rd Bussinello/Todare Alfa Romeo Giulia TZ, and 4th Kim/Thiele (Alfa Romeo Guilia TZ). Barth/Maglioli finished in 5th place and the first AC Cobra was that of Gurney/Grant in 8th place.

Le Mans

Three Prototype 4.2 litre V8 Lola-Fords were entered by Ford in 1964, to be driven by Phil Hill/McLaren, Ginther/Gregory, and Schlessor/Attwood and, to compete with the GT Ferraris, there were three 4.7 litre V8 Ford engined AC Cobras driven by Sears/Bolton, Gurney/Bondurant and Amon/Neerpasch. Ferrari had two 4 litre 330P for Surtees/Bandini and Graham Hill/Bonnier, and 3.3 litre 275Ps for Guichet/Vaccarella, Parkes/Scarfiotti and Baghetti/Maglioli. There were also two V8 Porsche 904s, a 5 litre Maserati and an Aston Martin DB4GT.

At the start the Ferraris of Surtees, Graham Hill and Rodriguez led but they were all passed by Ginther's Lola-Ford who later was forced to surrender his advantage when a pit stop for fuel was bungled. In the hours that followed the Lola-Ford of Phil Hill/McLaren closed on the leading Ferraris and was third overall when it stopped and retired with gearbox trouble on Sunday morning. Gearbox deficiencies had already claimed the other Fords so that the leading Ferraris of Guichet/Vaccarella and Surtees/Bonnier were unchallenged. Amongst the GT cars the AC Cobra of Gurney/Bondurant was out in front and the Aston Martin of Salmon/Sutcliffe lay third behind the second Cobra. Guichet/Vaccarella won at a record average speed of 121.56 mph. Next came the Surtees/Bandini Ferrari and in 3rd place the Gurney/Bondurant AC Cobra.

The Aston Martin DB4GT, which had been driven by Salmon/Sutcliffe was disqualified in the 19th hour for stopping for oil, having at one point been in 11th place. The Austin-Healey Sprite of Baker/Bradley finished 24th while the Lightweight E Type Jaguar of Lindner/Nocker retired in the 16th hour. A similar E Type, driven by Lumsden/Sargent retired in the 8th hour with gearbox trouble. A Lotus Elan driven by Gelee/Richard retired in the 3rd hour with overheating, and a Lotus Elite driven by Hunt/Wagstaff was placed 22nd. The MGB of Hopkirk/Hedges finished in 19th place of three Triumph Spitfires driven by Hobbs, Slotemaker, Tullius/Rothschild and Piot/Marnat, the first finished in 21st place while the other two retired after crashing.

Opposite, top: The Norinder/Troberg Ferrari 250 GTO racing to ninth place in the 1964 Targo Florio.

Opposite, bottom: The Cesare Topetti/Umberto Grana Ferrari GTO/64 being pursued by the Luigi Ravetto/Prince Gaetano Starrabba Ferrari 275LM during the Targa Florio.

The Surtees/Bandini 4 litre 330P Ferrari speeding towards third place at Le Mans in 1964 with John Surtees at the wheel.

1965
The top score again for Jim Clark

Bruce McLaren

The year 1965 was to be the last year of the 1.5 litre Formula which, in spite of being bitterly opposed before its introduction, had proved to be a great success. For 1965 Coventry-Climax produced a 32 valve V8 engine which was more powerful and also proved to be more than reliable than the one it replaced. An entirely new flat 16 engine had been promised by Coventry-Climax but it failed to be delivered through lack of resources. Ferrari had the flat 12 which had appeared at Monza in 1964 while B.R.M, with its sights firmly set on the 1966 3 litre Formula, made few changes to its cars. Jim Clark would drive the improved Lotus 33 while Graham Hill would be joined at B.R.M. by Jackie Stewart, Ritchie Ginther having left B.R.M. to drive the new Honda RA 272. The teams could choose Dunlop or Goodyear types in 1965. Rob Walker's drivers for 1965 would be Joakim Bonnier and Jo Siffert, and Masten Gregory would drive for Centro Sud.

The World Championship Series

South African Grand Prix: January 1

All the cars that arrived at East London were little changed from the previous Season, so recently ended, but Jackie Stewart was with Graham Hill in making his debut at B.R.M. for his first World Championship race. Jochen Rindt was with Bruce McLaren in the works Cooper team. Thankfully the Ferraris were painted red again but they were officially entered by Dragoni instead of Enzo Ferrari, who was still lacking a competition licence. Rob Walker had a Brabham-Climax for Joakim Bonnier and a Brabham-B.R.M. for Jo Siffert.

Jim Clark stamped his authority on the Grand Prix scene by putting up the fastest lap in practice in his Lotus 33. John Surtees was second fastest in a V8 Ferrari and Jack Brabham completed the front row of the grid in his Brabham-Climax. Next came Clark's team mate Mike Spence and Graham Hill's B.R.M. Lorenzo Bandini's Flat 12 Ferrari was 6th, Bonnier in Rob Walker's Brabham-Climax 7th, Bruce McLaren's Cooper-Climax 8th and newcomer Jackie Stewart 11th in the second B.R.M.

At the fall of the flag Clark established an immediate lead from his team mate Spence who in turn was followed by Brabham, McLaren, Surtees and Hill. The leading pair steadily drew away from the field and each other, while Surtees and Hill passed McLaren's Cooper-Climax. Bob Anderson (Brabham-Climax) was delayed with brake trouble and Dan Gurney's (Brabham-Climax) retired on lap 12 with ignition problems. Jackie Stewart was in 8th place behind the second Ferrari until Bandini lost time in his pit with electrical troubles. Spence spun at Beacon Bend on laps 43 and 60, as he had done during practice, allowing Surtees and Hill to pass him too. After leading from start to finish in this first race of the Season, **Clark won at 97.970 mph** from Surtees, Hill and Spence. Stewart finished 6th, scoring his first World Championship point in his very first outing with the B.R.M. Clark, who established the fastest lap of the race at 100.097 mph, had started as he intended to carry on.

Monaco Grand Prix: May 30

Neither Jim Clark nor Dan Gurney appeared at Monaco because they were in America to compete in the famous Indianapolis 500 Mile Race the next day. Clark would win it in his Type 29 Lotus-Ford after leading 190 of the 200 laps and his performance would bring about a revolution in the design of future Indianapolis 500 cars. Pedro Rodriguez was to have replaced Clark at Monaco but Lotus decided to withdraw from the race when guaranteed starts were only given to previous winners. Significantly, Denny Hume was given Gurney's place at Brabham and he was 8th in practice. Graham Hill's B.R.M, which had a revised exhaust system, was in pole position alongside Jack Brabham's car which had a new 32 valve Coventry-Climax engine. 3rd fastest was Jackie Stewart's B.R.M, revealing

The Ferraris of Lorenzo Bandini and John Surtees leading the eventual winner at Monaco in 1965.

John Surtees in his Tipo 158
Ferrari during the Monaco
Grand Prix.

Ronnie Bucknum in the new
Honda RA272 at Monaco.

its driver's potential, and Lorenzo Bandini's flat 12 Ferrari was 4th. Then came John Surtees (V8 Ferrari) and Richard Attwood Lotus-B.R.M. Two improved RA272 Hondas, driven by Ronnie Bucknum and Richie Ginther were on the 8th and last row of the grid in 15th and 16th places. Jochen Rindt, who would of course feature prominently in later years, failed to qualify for the race in a Cooper-Climax.

The two B.R.Ms of Hill and Stewart led away from the start followed by the Ferraris of Bandini and Surtees and Brabham's Brabham-Climax, none of which being able to match the pace of the cars from Bourne. Then on lap 30 Hill's progress was rudely interrupted when he came upon Bob Anderson's Brabham-Climax driving slowly through the chicane with mechanical problems. The B.R.M. took to the escape road and was then pushed back to the circuit by its driver to slot into 5th place. This put Stewart in the lead for the first time in a World Championship Grand Prix but a spin dropped him back to 4th place behind Bandini, Surtees and Brabham and just in front of his team mate Hill. Stewart allowed Hill to overtake him while, up at the front, Brabham now led. Brabham, whose rev counter had failed, retired in consequence with a blown engine on lap 43 and after this the two B.R.Ms only had the Ferraris with which to contend. Hill passed first Surtees and then Bandini but Surtees proceeded to pass his team mate and set after Hill. Then, on the penultimate lap Surtees coasted to a stop out of fuel so **the race ended with Hill's B.R.M. winning at a speed of 74.339 mph** from Bandini and Stewart. Denny Hulme was eighth in his first World Championship race. Hill also established the fastest lap of the race at 76.719 mph.

The Belgian Grand Prix: June 13

Jim Clark's Lotus 33 had a 32 valve Coventry-Climax engine at Spa, but Graham Hill was fastest in practice with his B.R.M. and Clark found himself to be sandwiched between the B.R.Ms of Hill and Jackie Stewart at the front of the grid. In a surprise 4th place was Richie Ginther's Honda and next came Dan Gurney's Brabham-Climax. The V8 Ferrari of John Surtees was 6th and the Flat 12 of Lorenzo Bandini only 17th. Ronnie Bucknum (Honda) was 11th and Jochen Rindt (Cooper-Climax) 14th.

The race started in heavy rain and Clark overtook Hill to lead during the first lap. Then

Jim Clark proving his mastery in his Lotus 33 in the rain at Spa.

came Stewart, ably supporting his team mate, and he was followed by Surtees, Ginther, Bruce McLaren (Cooper-Climax), Joakim Bonnier (Brabham-Climax), Gurney (Brabham-Climax) and Jack Brabham (Brabham-Climax). Clark put some distance between himself and Hill who was overtaken in the driving rain and blinding spray by Stewart on lap 4. Surtees took third place briefly, only to stop with engine trouble, and behind Clark and Stewart were Hill's B.R.M, McLaren's Cooper-Climax and Ginther's Honda. McLaren overtook Hill who was unhappy with his car and Brabham followed suit. Richard Attwood hit a telegraph pole in his Lotus-B.R.M. and escaped with minor burns when his car caught fire. The two young Scotsmen up at the front appeared to be undeterred by the rain and, in a race of their own, lapped the entire field. Clark had enough time in hand to be able to nurse his car with a slipping clutch over the last two laps. **Clark's winning average speed was 117.159 mph** and after Stewart, whose performance had been impressive, came McLaren, Brabham, Hill, and Ginther. It was a promising performance for Honda. The fastest lap of the race was Clark's at 124.716 mph.

French Grand Prix: June 27

Clark was already imposing his dominance and that of his Lotus-Climax on the 1965 Season and he was fastest in practice at Clermont-Ferrand. Jackie Stewart's B.R.M. was second on the starting grid and in front of World Champion Graham Hill. The other drivers must have been wondering what could be done about these two amazing Scotsmen! Next came the Ferraris of Lorenzo Bandini and John Surtees. Graham Hill was only 13th fastest after he had crashed heavily in practice when the throttle had stuck open on his spare car. Richie Ginther's Honda was in 7th place, Jochen Rindt's Cooper-Climax 12th. Ronnie Bucknum's Honda was on the back row in 16th place.

Clark led again at the start, according to his custom, and on this occasion from Bandini, Stewart, Dan Gurney and Surtees. By the end of the third lap Bandini had been overtaken by Stewart, who was to hold on to that position to the end. Dan Gurney (Brabham-Climax) and Surtees followed in 4th and 5th places, while Clark extended his lead. Gurney dropped back and eventually retired on lap 17 with engine trouble. Mike Spence lost time with a faulty fuel pump and Surtees was delayed with mechanical problems. Bandini spun and crashed three laps from the end of the race. Graham Hill had been plagued with clutch trouble from the beginning and remained in a lowly place to finish 5th one lap down. **It was Clark's race at 89.216 mph** and he finished 26 seconds ahead of Stewart's B.R.M.

Jim Clark leading from start to finish in the French Grand Prix.

Surtees (V8 Ferrari) was 3rd, Denny Hulme (Brabham-Climax) 4th and Hill (B.R.M.) 5th. The fastest lap was again recorded by Clark at 90.590 mph.

British Grand Prix: July 10

Jim Clark was again fastest in practice with his 32 valve Coventry-Climax engined Lotus 33. Graham Hill, reasserting his position in the team after the French Grand Prix, was just 0.2 second slower in his B.R.M. and the front row of the grid was completed by Richer Ginther's Honda and Jackie Stewart's B.R.M. The Ferraris of John Surtees and Lorenzo Bandini were 5th and 9th, Surtees now driving the Flat 12 cylinder car. Dan Gurney was 7th with a 32 valve Climax engine in his Brabham.

Starting Grid

J. Stewart	P.R. Ginther	G. Hill	J. Clark
B.R.M	Honda	B.R.M	Lotus-Climax
1 min 31.3 secs	1 min 31.3 secs	1 min 31.0 secs	1 min 30.8 secs

D. Gurney	M. Spence	J. Surtees
Brabham-Climax	Lotus-Climax	Ferrari
1 min 31.9 secs	1 min 31.7 secs	1 min 31.3 secs

B. McLaren	D. Hulme	L. Bandini	J. Brabham
Cooper-Climax	Brabham-Climax	Ferrari	Brabham-Climax
1 min 32.8 secs	1 min 31.7 secs	1 min 32.7 secs	1 min 32.5 secs

J. Bonnier	F. Gardner	J. Rindt
Brabham-Climax	Brabham-B.R.M	Cooper-Climax
1 min 33.5 secs	1 min 33.4 secs	1 min 32.9 secs

J. Siffert	R. Anderson	R. Attwood	I. Ireland
Brabham-B.R.M	Brabham-Climax	Lotus-B.R.M	Lotus-B.R.M
1 min 34.2 secs	1 min 34.1 secs	1 min 33.8 secs	1 min 33.6 secs

J. Rhodes	I. Raby	M. Gregory
Cooper-Climax	Brabham-B.R.M	B.R.M
1 min 39.4 secs	1 min 36.0 secs	1 min 35.9 secs

Dan Gurney's latest Coventry-Climax engine failed comprehensively on the warm up lap and so he switched to Jack Brabham's car instead. History was made at the start as it was the white and red Japanese Honda that led the field in the hands of Richie Ginther. However the Honda was quickly overtaken by Clark on the first lap and both Graham Hill and John Surtees followed him on the second. Jackie Stewart was behind Ginther and the five kept to that order as Clark and Hill drew steadily away. Then the Honda developed a misfire and fell back to retire on lap 27. Denny Hulme (Brabham-Climax) retired with a broken alternator belt on lap 30 but the order at the front remained unchanged. Then on lap 60 Clark's engine struck an uncertain note. He was 35 seconds ahead of Hill and this was reduced to 25 seconds ten laps later with ten more to go. With falling oil pressure he managed to nurse the car home, watching his mirrors all the time, and finished just 3.2 seconds ahead of Hill. **Clark won the race at 112.020 mph.** The fastest lap was recorded by Hill at 114.285 mph on lap 80 when he was desperately trying to reduce the deficit. Stewart finished in fifth place in his B.R.M.

Jochen Rindt in his works Cooper-Climax during the British Grand Prix at Silverstone.

Results

1. J. Clark	Lotus–Climax	2 hr 05 min 25.4 secs
2. G. Hill	B.R.M	2 hr 05 min 28.6 secs
3. J. Surtees	Ferrari	2 hr 05 min 53.0 secs
4. M. Spence	Lotus–Climax	2 hr 06 min 05.0 secs
5. J. Stewart	B.R.M	2 hr 06 min 40.0 secs
6. D. Gurney	Brabham–Climax	1 lap.
7. J. Bonnier	Brabham–Climax	
8. F. Gardner	Brabham–B.R.M	2 laps
9. J. Siffert	Brabham–B.R.M	
10. B. McLaren	Cooper–Climax	3 laps
11. I. Raby	Brabham–B.R.M	7 laps
12. M. Gregory	B.R.M	10 laps
13. R. Attwood	Lotus–B.R.M	17 laps
14. J. Rindt	Cooper–Climax	18 laps

Retirements

L. Bandini (Ferrari) lap 3 engine, P.R. Ginther (Honda) lap 27 ignition, D. Hulme

(Brabham-Climax) lap 30 alternator belt, R. Anderson (Brabham-Climax) lap 34 gearbox, J. Rhodes (Cooper-Climax) lap 39 ignition, I. Ireland (Lotus-B.R.M.) lap 42 engine.

Dutch Grand Prix: July 18

Graham Hill's B.R.M. was fastest throughout practice at Zandvoort and he spent some time experimenting with different Dunlop tyre options. Jim Clark opted for the 16 valve Lotus-Climax at Zandvoort after his 32 valve engine had developed an oil leak. He was 2nd fastest and had Richie Ginther's Honda alongside him in 3rd place. After them came John Surtees (Ferrari), Dan Gurney (Brabham-Climax) and Jackie Stewart (B.R.M.)

It was Ginther who made the best start of the race again and he was followed by Hill and Clark. Hill got past the Honda to lead on lap 2 and Clark went from third to first in the following three laps. Ginther slipped back through the field while Gurney (Brabham-Climax) assumed 3rd place, pursued by Stewart's B.R.M, Surtees' Ferrari, Mike Spence's Lotus-Climax and Denny Hulme's Brabham-Climax. Gurney closed on Hill while Clark steadily extended his lead and after Gurney passed Hill the B.R.M. driver let his team mate through as his rev counter had failed. By lap 32 Stewart was ahead of Gurney but could do nothing about **Clark who won the race from Stewart** at 100.865 mph after establishing the fastest lap at 103.525 mph. After Stewart and Gurney came Hill, Hulme, Ginther and Surtees.

There had been drama before the race when Colin Chapman was arrested after a confrontation with the overzealous Dutch police but he was released without charge!

German Grand Prix: August 1

There were no Hondas at the Nurburgring as the Japanese team was taking a breather before Monza. The front row of the grid consisted of Jim Clark (Lotus-32 valve Climax), Jackie Stewart (B.R.M.), Graham Hill (B.R.M.) and John Surtees (Ferrari). Stewart's performance was remarkable bearing in mind he had never been on the challenging circuit before.

Once again it was Clark who made the best start while Surtees was left behind with gear selection difficulties. Behind Clark were the B.R.Ms of Hill and Stewart and Dan Gurney's Brabham-Climax. Clark broke the lap record on laps 1 and 2 and then Clark and Hill jointly broke the record again on lap 3. Stewart retired after bending his suspension on the third lap. Behind Clark, Hill and Gurney were gradually slipping back and 4th place was contested by a host of cars. After the retirement of Chris Amon (Lotus-B.R.M.) with an ignition problem on lap 4, Denny Hulme (Brabham-Climax) with a fuel leak on lap 6, Bruce McLaren (Cooper-Climax) with gearbox problem on lap 8, and Mike Spence (Lotus-Climax) with a broken driveshaft on lap 9, it was Jochen Rindt who firmly laid claim to the fourth slot.

Clark won at 99.756 mph. Remarkably, it was his sixth win in the first six World Championship events in 1965 and it assured him of his second World Championship. Hill (B.R.M.) was 2nd, 15.9 seconds behind and, Gurney (Brabham-Climax), who had been steadily closing on the B.R.M. in the latter stages of the race, was 3rd. Jochen Rindt (Cooper-Climax) was 4th and Jack Brabham (Brabham-Climax) 5th., Lorenzo Bandini (V8 Ferrari) 6th, Masten Gregory (Centro Sud B.R.M.) 8th and one lap behind. Clark established the fastest lap of the race at 101.219 mph.

Italian Grand Prix: September 12

The Hondas were back at Monza after undergoing development work since the Dutch Grand Prix. Their engines had been lowered and, consequently, their handling qualities improved. Ronnie Bucknum was 6th fastest but Richie Ginther could only manage 17th place on the grid after he had an engine blow up during practice. Jim Clark, with the 32 valve V8 engine installed in his Lotus-Climax, was again in pole with John Surtees (Ferrari) and Jackie Stewart (B.R.M.) sharing the front row with him. Graham Hill (B.R.M.) and

Lorenzo Bandini (Ferrari) were in the second row. There were four Ferraris for Surtees, Bandini, Nino Vaccarella and Ludovico Scaffiotti.

At the start Surtees' Ferrari faltered with clutch trouble while Graham Hill shot forward from the second row between Clark and Surtees to lead the race. However, by the end of the first lap the order was Stewart and Clark, both racing side by side, followed by Hill, Bandini, Siffert (Brabham-B.R.M.), Spence (Lotus-Climax) and Gurney (Brabham-Climax). Once he got going Surtees made rapid progress through the field in an effort to catch up with the leaders. Clark, Stewart and Hill were all close together and constantly exchanging the lead while Dan Gurney (Brabham-Climax), Lorenzo Bandini and Mike Spence (Lotus-Climax) were in an equally fluid situation. Any one of Clark, Stewart and Hill might have been leading the race on any given lap while Surtees, in spite of his valiant efforts, finally retired with clutch trouble on lap 35. Clark also dropped out on lap 63 through the failure of his fuel pump, having shared the lead with the two B.R.Ms for so much of the race. Hill and Stewart intended to end the race in close formation but then Hill lost a few seconds at the Parabolica on the last lap so that the race **provided Jackie Stewart with his first World Championship win at 130.464 mph.** Hill (B.R.M.) was 2nd Gurney (Brabham-Climax) 3rd Bandini (Ferrari) 4th and Bruce McLaren (Cooper-Climax) 5th. The fastest lap of the race was credited to Clark at 133.427 mph.

United States Grand Prix: October 3

With John Surtees recovering from an injury incurred during practice for a sports car race in Canada the previous week Ferrari's hopes at Watkins Glen rested mainly with Lorenzo Bandini, although Pedro Rodriquez and Bob Bondurant drove two additional Ferraris entered by N.A.R.T. Jim Clark's Lotus again had the 32 valve engine but Dan Gurney's succumbed to oil leaks forcing him to use the 16 valve version instead. There was an additional works Lotus for Moises Solana. Jackie Stewart soon mastered Watkins Glen, this being his first experience of the circuit, but Graham Hill's B.R.M. was fastest at the end of practice with Jim Clark's Lotus-Climax next to it on the front row of the grid. Richie Ginther's Honda was 3rd fastest. Bandini's Ferrari and Stewart's B.R.M. were 5th and 6th.

As the field settled down after the start the order became Hill, Clark and Stewart, with Ginther dropping back from third place in the scrum. Stewart's suspension was damaged when he was forced off the road but he maintained his pace and stayed with the two cars ahead of him until he lost time at his pit to have his throttle cable repaired. Hill and Clark

Graham Hill winning the 1965 United States Grand Prix at Watkins Glen in his B.R.M.

remained in close company but on lap 12 Clark was forced to give up the chase as he stopped with a broken piston. Mike Spence's Lotus-Climax retired on lap 10 (engine), Innes Ireland's Lotus-B.R.M. also stopped on lap 10 because its driver was unwell. Bruce McLaren's Cooper-Climax was out on lap 12 with failing oil pressure. Behind Hill's B.R.M. the Brabhams of Jack Brabham and Dan Gurney contested 2rd place and Lorenzo Bandini followed them at a distance. Then on lap 37 Hill's B.R.M. was suddenly blown off course by a violent gust of wind and this enabled Brabham to reduce his lead and Jack managed to slipped past Hill when the B.R.M. was held up by Richard Attwood's Lotus-B.R.M. However Brabham's lead was short lived as Hill was soon past him again when he went wide on a bend. **Hill won the race by 12 seconds at 107.977 mph** from Gurney, Brabham, Bandini, Pedro Rodriquez (Ferrari), Jochen Rindt (Cooper-Climax) and Ginther. Hill was also responsible for the fastest lap of the race at 115.157 mph.

Mexican Grand Prix: October 24

Jackie Stewart had to use the spare B.R.M. for the race in Mexico City after engine and suspension failures during practice. Jim Clark (Lotus-Climax) was fastest ahead of Dan Gurney's Brabham-Climax and Richie Ginther's Honda. Then came Jack Brabham (Brabham-Climax), Graham Hill (B.R.M.), Mike Spence (Lotus-Climax), Lorenzo Bandini (Ferrari) and Jackie Stewart's B.R.M. Both works Brabhams had 16 valve engines as the team's 32 valve engine had proved to be unreliable.

Richie Ginther shot into the lead, closely followed by Jackie Stewart, up from the fourth row of the grid. After these came Spence, Gurney, Bandini, Brabham and Hill.

Jim Clark was forced to pull out of the race on lap 9 with engine trouble and Stewart began to fall back with a slipping clutch. Brabham was delayed by several minutes for essential mechanical repairs. Ginther had maintained a clear lead from the first lap of the race and behind him on lap 11 were Spence, Hill and Gurney. On the next lap Gurney overtook Hill and on lap 17 he passed Spence into 2nd place. Behind Hill were Stewart, Bandini and Rodriguez. Then Bandini came into his pit after denting his car on the circuit markers and Rodriguez pitted with a misfire. Siffert then inherited 4th place when Stewart was finally forced to retire on account of his clutch. Hill was also out on lap 57 with a blown engine, and so **Ginther scored Honda's first World Championship win** in the last race for the 1.5 litre Formula at 94.262 mph. Gurney (Brabham-Climax) was 2nd. Spence (Lotus-Climax) 3rd Jo Siffert (Brabham-Climax) 4th and Ronnie Buckman (Honda) 5th. The fastest lap of the race was achieved by Gurney at 96.553 mph.

The World Championship

Jim Clark was the clear winner of the World Championship with six wins and 54 points. Graham Hill was 2nd with 40 and Jackie Stewart 3rd with 33. Then came Dan Gurney with 25 points, John Surtees with 17, Lorenzo Bandini with 13 and Richie Ginther with 11.

The Constructors' World Championship was won by Lotus-Ford with 54 points. Then came B.R.M. with 45, Brabham-Ford with 27, Ferrari with 26, Cooper-Climax with 14, Honda with 11, Brabham-B.R.M. with 5 and Lotus-B.R.M. with 2.

The Brands Hatch Race of Champions

This was the first international Formula 1 race in 1965 and, run in two 40 lap heats, attracted a good entry.

The front row of the grid for Heat 1 consisted of Jim Clark (Lotus 33), Graham Hill (B.R.M.) and Mike Spence (Lotus 33). Behind these came Joakim Bonnier (Rob Walker Brabham-Climax) and Jack Brabham (Brabham-Climax). Jackie Stewart (B.R.M.) was 6th and John Surtees 7th in a lone V8 Ferrari.

Clark shot away from the start followed by his team mate and after these came Hill, Surtees, who was unhappy with his car, and Stewart. Dan Gurney (Brabham-Climax)

John Surtees unhappy with his Ferrari during the 1965 Race of Champions at Brands Hatch.

caught up from the fifth row to take second place behind Clark and, at the end of the Heat the order was Clark, Gurney, Spence, Brabham, Hill, Surtees and Stewart.

At the beginning of Heat II Clark led again from Gurney and the two left the rest far behind. Clark fought long and hard to keep Gurney at bay but, having taken to the grass to avoid him, crashed heavily over an earth bank to retire unhurt. Soon after this Gurney was out of the race with engine trouble and it was Brabham who led from Spence, Hill and Stewart. Hill then retired with an overheating engine and Surtees stopped with engine trouble. The Heat was won by Spence from Bonnier, Gardner (Brabham-B.R.M.) and Stewart.

The overall result was a win for Spence with Stewart coming 2nd, Bonnier 3rd, and Gardner 4th.

Monte Carlo Rally

The competitors in 1965 Monte Carlo Rally experienced the most severe weather conditions with blizzards, deep snow drifts, glacial ice flows and obscured road signs. They were the kind of conditions for which the Rally was intended. Of the 237 starters only 35 finished each stage within the permitted time limit, and only 22 cars completed the 380 mile high speed test on the mountains above Monte Carlo within the half hour allowed after the required finishing time. There were BMC Minis, Austin 1800s, Triumph Spitfires, Rover 2000s and Ford Cortinas. Six Saabs, four Minis and two Austin 1800s were amongst the 35 finishers in Monte Carlo. The winners were Timo Makinen and Paul Easter in a Mini Cooper S. In second place came Eugen Bohringer and Rolf Wutherick in a Porsche. The Coupe des Dames was won again by Pat Moss who also came third in the Rally in a Mini Cooper.

Timo Makinen and Paul Easter
on their way to winning the
1965 Monte Carlo Rally.

Targa Florio

Abarth had a new car based on the Fiat 850 with a 1,600 cc twin cam engine for
Herrmann/Cella. Aaltonen/Baker drove an Austin Healey Sprite and Porsche had two
914 Coupes, a flat eight for Bonnier/Graham Hill and a flat 6 for Maglioli/Linge. There
was also a new eight cylinder Porsche for Davis/Mitter. Ferrari was back with three works
275P/2s with 3.3 litre V12 engines for Vaccarella/Bandini, Scarfiotti/Parkes and Guichet/
Baghetti. There was also a works GTB to be driven by Biscaldi/Deserti. Ford had a GT
Prototype with a 4.7 litre V8 engine for Sir John Whitmore/Bondurant and there was also
a number of Alfa Romeo Giulia TZ Coupes in the line up.

By the second lap the order was Vaccarella, Mairesse and Scarfiotti, with Bonnier sixth
and Davis ninth. The Bonnier/Graham Hill Porsche was delayed with throttle problems
and the Ford lost a wheel. Vaccarella/Bandini continued to lead, now from Guichet/
Baghetti and Maglioli/Linge. On lap seven the Guichet/Baghetti Ferrari stopped with a

The Nino Vaccarella/Lorenzo
Bandini 275P2 Ferrari winning
the 1965 Targa Florio.

broken battery, but the Vaccarella/Bandini continued until the end to win the 49th Targa Florio. 2nd was the Davis/Mitter Porsche, 3rd the Maglioli/Linge 6 cylinder Porsche, 4th the Bonnier/Graham Hill Porsche and 5th the 914 GTS of Klaas/Pucci. Of the 59 starters 29 finished before the roads were re opened again to the public.

Le Mans

Eleven Fords opposed eleven Ferraris at Le Mans in 1965 and they faced the possible intervention of a 5 litre V8 "birdcage" Maserati, two 8 cylinder Porsches and a 6 cylinder Porsche. There was also the Rover–B.R.M, driven by Graham Hill/Stewart. The mighty 7 litre Ford GT40s of McLaren and Amon streaked away from the field at the beginning but they would be handicapped by having to stop for fuel more frequently than the other cars. The Phil Hill/Amon car broke the lap record at 141.5 mph but five Ferraris were in

The 7 litre Ford Mk II of Bruce McLaren and Ken Miles leading at Le Mans until it retired.

The Phil Hill/Bruce McLaren Ford GT40 being followed by the Salmon/Sutcliffe Aston Martin DB4GT at Le Mans.

command of the race after three hours. The Fords were retiring with gearbox problems although the Phil Hill/Amon car kept going some way down the field, continuing to lower the lap record until its clutch failed. The Surtees/Scarfiotti Ferrari led into the night but the Surtees/Scarfiotti car was held at the pits with a broken front suspension. Brake troubles afflicted the works Ferraris and it was left to the private entrants to uphold the honour of Italy. The AC Cobras were also in trouble and it was the 275LM Ferraris of Gregory/Rindt and Dumay/Gosselin which finished in the first two places, Mairesse/Beurlys being 3rd in a 275GTB. The Porsches were 4th and 5th and the Rover-B.R.M. turbine car was 10th and the best placed British car!

The Hopkirk/Hedges MGB was 11th, the Hawkins/Rhodes Austin-Healey Sprite 12th, the Thuner/Lampinen Triumph Spitfire 13th, and the Piot/Dubois Triumph Spitfire 14th.

The Masten Gregory/Jochen Rindt 250LM Ferrari winning the 1965 Le Mans 24 Hour Race.

The Rover-B.R.M. of Graham Hill and Jackie Stewart at Le Mans in 1965.

1966
The big beasts are back

The success of the 1.5 litre Formula had been due in large measure to Coventry-Climax who provided competitive engines for Lotus, Cooper and Brabham, but all these constructors were faced with a major problem in 1966 as Coventry-Climax had announced that it would withdraw from motor racing for financial reasons. The solution was found by Colin Chapman who persuaded Walter Hayes of the Ford Motor Company to finance the production of a new 3 litre DFV (Double Four Valve) V8 engine by Keith Duckworth and Mike Costin of Cosworth Engineering. Time would reveal that it would be responsible for 155 wins between 1967 and 1983. However interim measures were necessary and Coventry-Climax agreed to produce a 2 litre version of their V8 for the 1965 Lotus 33. Chapman also adopted the new H16 B.R.M. engine for his Lotus 43, Jim Clark giving the engine its only win. John Cooper gained an agreement from Maserati which meant that the Italian firm would provide 3 litre V12 engines for the Cooper Team and he produced a monocoque to accommodate it. Jack Brabham persuaded the Australian firm Repco to build a fuel injected 3 litre V8 engine based on an obsolete aluminium V8 Oldsmobile block and Ron Tauranac built a multi- tubular space frame car for it in time for the start of the season. In addition Brabham had at his disposal the early 4 cylinder 2.5 litre Coventry-Climax engines. Honda produced a 3 litre V12 engine for a new stressed skin monocoque which housed no less than nine fuel tanks, strategically positioned to most effectively distribute their weight, and this made its debut at Monza. Bruce McLaren decided to follow Jack Brabham's example in building his own car, using an Indianapolis V8 Ford engine reduced to 3 litres fitted into a monocoque designed by Robin Herd and made of Malite. Dan Gurney also built his own car of monocoque construction which was designed by Len Terry and called the Eagle. He used an old 4 cylinder Coventry-Climax engine of 2.7 litres until an entirely new V12 engine designed by Aubrey Woods, formerly of B.R.M. and built by Weslake in Rye, Sussex. Ferrari, always strong on engines, was well prepared for the new Formula with a V12 fuel injected engine reduced from 3.3 to 3 litres and fitted to a semi monocoque for John Surtees and Lorenzo Bandini. Finally B.R.M. produced from two 1.5 litre V8 engines a 3 litre H16, mounting one on top of the other, and fitted to the P83. It seemed a good idea at the time but B.R.M. would encounter serious development problems as the H16 was comparatively heavy and prone to oil leaks. B.R.M. used their V8 enlarged to 2 litres until the H16 was deemed to be serviceable. Reg Parnell Racing's 2 litre B.R.M. engined Lotus 25s would be driven by Mike Spence and Richard Attwood while Graham Hill and Jackie Stewart continued to be B.R.Ms work's drivers.

Jochen Rindt.

Monaco Grand Prix: May 22

The new 3 litre Cooper-Maseratis arrived at Monaco for the first race of the Season as did also the entirely new McLaren which was at this stage finished in white with a green and silver strip and powered by a 3 litre Indianapolis V8 Ford engine. Bandini had the option of a 3 litre V12 Ferrari or the earlier car with a 2.4 litre V6 engine. B.R.M. brought an H16 P83 for Graham Hill to test during practice but used two Tasman Series 2 litre V8s for the race. Lotus had an untried and untested H16 B.R.M. engine but Jim Clark used a 2 litre V8 Coventry-Climax engine for the race. Mike Spence drove Tim Parnell's Lotus and Mike Spence Rob Walker's Brabham, each having 2 litre V8 B.R.M. engines. Clark still managed pole position in spite of his car suffering a broken crown wheel and pinion during practice. John Surtees was next to him with his 2.4 litre V6 Ferrari. Then came the

Jackie Stewart winning the Monaco Grand Prix in the 2 litre V8 B.R.M.

John Surtees' 3 litre V12 Ferrari being pursued by Jackie Stewart's B.R.M. at Monaco.

B.R.Ms of Jackie Stewart and Graham Hill, followed by Lorenzo Bandini's V6 Ferrari and Denny Hulme's Brabham-Climax. Bruce McLaren was 10th in practice with his McLaren-Ford but was to retire with an oil leak on the 4th lap of the race.

Clark was left behind at the start, stuck in first gear, and it was Surtees who led from Jackie Stewart who was in turn followed by Graham Hill (B.R.M.), Denny Hulme (Brabham-Repco), Jochen Rindt Cooper-Maserati), Bob Anderson (Brabham-Climax), Lorenzo Bandini (V6 Ferrari), Bruce McLaren (McLaren-Ford) and Mike Spence (Lotus-B.R.M.). Surtees was pushed hard by Stewart and he waved the Scotsman past on lap 16, dropping back to retire the following lap with a broken rear axle. Stewart now had a clear lead from Jochen Rindt (Cooper-Maserati), Hill (B.R.M.) and Bandini (Ferrari), but Bandini then overtook both Hill and Rindt and Rindt slowed to retire with engine trouble. Meanwhile Clark was slicing through the field from the back to challenge Hill for 3rd place. He had in fact passed Hill when his race was ended suddenly on lap 61 due to a broken rear suspension. Hill spun, dropping a long way back from Bandini and **Stewart won with 40.2 seconds to spare** from Bandini (Ferrari), Hill (B.R.M.) and Bob Bondurant (B.R.M.). Stewart's record average speed for the race was 76.515 mph, and the fastest lap was recorded by Bandini at 78.342 mph.

Belgian Grand Prix: June 12

The Belgian Grand Prix witnessed the debut of Dan Gurney's Eagle with its interim 4 cylinder 2.7 litre Coventry-Climax engine. Peter Arundell tried the H16 B.R.M. engine in the new Lotus 43 and encountered mechanical problems while Jim Clark chose to drive a Lotus 33 with a 2 litre Coventry-Climax engine. Clark could only manage 10th in practice and was alongside Graham Hill's 2 litre B.R.M. on the 4th row of the grid. Bruce McLaren had a 3 litre V8 McLaren-Serenissima while his Ford engine was being modified. The Serenissima engine was designed by Maserati's former chief engineer Alberto Massimino but the car failed to make it to the start. John Surtees' 3 litre V12 Ferrari was fastest in practice and next came Jochen Rindt (Cooper-Maserati) Jackie Stewart (V8 B.R.M.) Jack Brabham (Brabham-Repco) and Lorenzo Bandini (V6 2.4 litre Ferrari.) Four different makes in the first four places, so the new Formula promised some highly competitive races. Dan Gurney's Eagle-Climax was back in 6th row in 15th place.

Clark's engine blew up within a hundred yards of the line but Surtees, in heavy rain, shot off into an early lead from Brabham and Bandini. Seven cars were missing at the end of

John Surtees' Tipo 312 Ferrari winning the 1966 Belgian Grand Prix.

John Surtees winning the
Belgian Grand Prix.

the first lap and there had been a number of spins and excursions which left Bob
Bondurant's B.R.M. upside down in a ditch, the driver fortunately avoiding serious injury.
Stewart's situation was much more perilous as he was left trapped in his car and soaked in
petrol leaking from a ruptured fuel tank. Hill and Bondurant went to Stewart's assistance,
and finally managed to free him from beneath his steering wheel with the aid of a spanner
borrowed from a spectator's tool bag on the other side of the track! This enabled Stewart,
who was suffering from a broken collar bone, dislocated shoulder, crushed ribs and
concussion, to be moved to a place of relative safety by the two racing drivers who laid
him down in a barn, watched by two nuns. The ambulance with its police escort eventually
conveyed him to Liege Hospital after managing to lose both its escort and its way en route!
Alfred Owen's brother in law Louis Stanley and Jim Clark went in the ambulance with
Stewart, and Stanley became as dedicated as Stewart to the cause of safety. The others who
crashed out in the rain on that first lap were Joakim Bonnier (Cooper-Maserati), Mike
Spence (Lotus-B.R.M.), Jo Siffert (Cooper-Maserati) and Denny Hulme (Brabham-
Climax). After the first three cars that completed that first lap came the Cooper-Maseratis
of Ginther, Rindt and Guy Ligier. Bandini overtook Brabham, and briefly passed Surtees,
while Rindt overtook Ginther, Brabham and Bandini. **John Surtees won the race at
113.934 mph.** Rindt was 2nd, Bandini 3rd. Brabham 4th and Ginther 5th. Surtees set the
fastest lap of the race at 121.920 mph.

As a result of Jackie Stewart's experience at Spa Louis Stanley, whose friendship I valued,
established the International Grand Prix Medical Service which, with its AEC lorry
equipped with an X ray machine and an operating theatre, was on hand at every race.

French Grand Prix: Rheims: July 3

Graham Hill had two P83 H16 B.R.Ms at his disposal for the high speed circuit of Rheims
but although everyone was impressed by their speed on the long straights he experienced

major problems in practice and opted to race a 2 litre V8 B.R.M. instead. John Surtees, having left Ferrari after a disagreement, had a works Cooper-Maserati on the front row of the grid, sandwiched between the V12 Ferraris of Lorenzo Bandini and Mike Parkes, the last named making his Grand Prix debut. Immediately behind them came Jack Brabham (Brabham-Repco) and Jochen Rindt (Cooper-Maserati) who had distinguished himself with his performance at Spa. In the absence of Jackie Stewart, who was recovering from Spa, Graham Hill's B.R.M. was 8th fastest alongside the Cooper-Maseratis of Jo Siffert and Chris Amon. Dan Gurney's Eagle-Climax was down in 14th place. Peter Arundell was back in the last row with his Lotus 43, plagued by trouble with its H16 engine while Jim Clark was forced to withdraw after being hit in his face by a bird during practice. Pedro Rodriquez put Clark's Lotus-B.R.M. in 13th place.

Surtees led initially with his Cooper-Maserati but slowed when his engine was starved of fuel thus letting Bandini into the lead, followed by Brabham and Parkes. Bandini repeatedly broke the lap record out in front while Arundell was stopped with gearbox problems. Graham Hill climbed several places until he was challenging Parkes for 3rd place but then his engine lost power and he was forced to retire on lap 14. Bandini was out on his own when his throttle cable broke on lap 37 and then his race was over. **Jack Brabham won the race at 136.987 mph,** well ahead of Parkes in 2nd place. The race was won at 136.987 mph. Denny Hulme (Brabham-Repco) was 3rd, Jochen Rindt (Cooper-Maserati) 4th, and Dan Gurney (Eagle-Climax) 5th. The fastest lap of the race was set by Bandini at 141.435 mph.

Mike Parkes taking his long chassis Ferrari to second place in the French Grand Prix in his introduction to Formula 1.

British Grand Prix: July 16

Industrial disputes in Italy led to the absence of Ferraris at Silverstone, and continuing problems with the H16 B.R.M. engine left Lotus with a borrowed 2 litre V8 B.R.M. engine and its own 2 litre Coventry-Climax unit. B.R.M. itself was dependent upon its V8 engined cars too and it was becoming clear that it would be a long haul to get the P83 cars both fast and reliable. Brabham had the advantage of his 3 litre Repco engines being both reliable and up to speed and this was demonstrated on the starting grid. Jack Brabham was in pole position and Denny Hulme 2nd fastest a full second ahead of Dan Gurney's Eagle-Climax. Jim Clark and Jackie Stewart had both recovered from their injuries and were in 5th and 8th places. A third works Brabham with a 2.5 litre Coventry-Climax engine was driven by Chris Irwin. Bruce McLaren had a new Serenissima engine as his Ford V8 was still not ready. Paul Emery produced a one off Shannon-Climax for Trevor Taylor and Pearce Engineering provided a Cooper with a V12 3 litre GTO Ferrari engine for Chris Lawrence to drive.

Starting Grid

D. Gurney	D. Hulme	J. Brabham
Eagle-Climax	Brabham-Repco	Brabham-Repco
1 min 35.8 secs	1 min 34.8 secs	1 min 34.5 secs

J. Clark	G. Hill
Lotus-Climax	B.R.M
1 min 36.1 secs	1 min 36.0 secs

J. Stewart	J. Rindt	J. Surtees
B.R.M	Cooper-Maserati	Cooper-Maserati
1 min 36 9 secs	1 min 36.6 secs	1 min 36.4 secs

R. Anderson	M. Spence
Brabham-Climax	Lotus-B.R.M
1 min 37.5 secs	1 min 37.3 secs

B. McLaren	C. Irwin	J. Siffert
McLaren-Serenissima	Brabham-Climax	Cooper-Maserati
1 min 38.5 secs	1 min 38.1 secs	1 min 38.0 secs

J. Bonnier	B. Bondurant
Brabham-Climax	B.R.M
1 min 39.3 secs	1 min 38.9 secs

T. Taylor	G. Ligier	J. Taylor
Shannon-Climax	Cooper-Maserati	Brabham-B.R.M.
1 min 41.6 secs	1 min 41.4 secs	1 min 40.0 secs

P. Arundell	C. Lawrence
Lotus-B.R.M	Cooper-Ferrari
1 min 54.3 secs	1 min 43.8 secs

Most of the drivers had changed from wet tyres when the conditions improved just before the race. This handed an initial advantage to the Cooper-Maseratis of Jochen Rindt and John Surtees as they were still on wets, but it was Jack Brabham (Brabham-Climax) and Dan Gurney (Eagle-Climax) who led from Jim Clark (Lotus-Climax) ,Rindt and Surtees. Both Cooper-Maseratis passed Clark, and Rindt also passed Gurney. Surtees followed him through as the Eagle slowed and retired on lap 9 with engine trouble. Rindt and Surtees now found themselves increasingly handicapped by the drying track and they were passed by Graham Hill (B.R.M.), Clark, and Denny Hulme (Brabham-Repco). Clark stopped at his pit for more brake fluid and, setting out again, caught up to 4th place before the end of the race. Hill slowed with falling oil pressure and **the race was a triumph for Jack Brabham** who won at 95.479 mph from Hume (Brabham Repco), Hill (B.R.M.) Clark (Lotus-Climax) and Rindt (Lotus-Climax. The fastest lap of the race was made by Brabham at 98.350 mph.

Opposite, top: John Surtees and Jochen Rindt in their 3 litre Cooper-Maseratis during the British Grand Prix at Brands Hatch.

Opposite, bottom: Jack Brabham's Brabham-Repco at Brands Hatch.

Signed painting of Jackie
Stewart in his 2 litre V8 B.R.M.
during the British Grand Prix.

Results

1. J. Brabham	Brabham-Repco	2 hr 13 min 13.4 secs
2. D. Hume	Brabham-Repco	2 hr 13 min 23.0 secs
3. G. Hill	B.R.M	1 lap
4. J. Clark	Lotus-Climax	
5. J. Rindt	Cooper-Maserati	
6. B. McLaren	McLaren-Serenissima	2 laps
7. C. Irwin	Brabham-Climax	
8. J. Taylor	Brabham-B.R.M	4 laps
9. B. Bondurant	B.R.M	
10. G. Ligier	Cooper-Maserati	5 laps
11. C. Lawrence	Cooper-Ferrari	7 laps

Still running: J. Siffert Cooper-Maserati 10 laps down, R. Anderson Brabham-Climax 10 laps down.

Retirements

T. Taylor Shannon-Climax lap 1 engine, D. Gurney Eagle-Climax lap 9 engine, M. Spence Lotus-B.R.M. lap 15 oil leak, J. Stewart B.R.M. lap 17 engine, P. Arundell Lotus-B.R.M. lap 32 gearbox, J. Bonnier Brabham-Climax lap 42 clutch, J. Surtees Cooper-Maserati lap 67 transmission.

Dutch Grand Prix: July 24

Ferrari was back at Zandvoort with Mike Parkes and Lorenzo Bandini but of course John Surtees was now with Cooper. Jack Brabham was in pole position again with his Brabham-Repco and Denny Hulme next to him again in his identical car. Jim Clark was 3rd in his Lotus-Climax V8. Dan Gurney (Eagle-2.7 litre 4 cylinder Climax) and Mike Parkes (V12 Ferrari) occupied the second row and Jochen Rindt's Cooper-Maserati led the V8 B.R.Ms of Graham Hill and Jackie Stewart in row three.

Brabham seized an instant advantage at the start of the race followed by Clark and Hulme but all three were virtually tied together for several laps. Hulme's Brabham-Repco was the first to fall away, with ignition problems and it was Gurney's Eagle-Climax that

Jack Brabham winning the Dutch Grand Prix in the 3 litre Brabham-Repco.

challenged Hill's B.R.M. for third place. Gurney was delayed at his pit and finally retired on lap 27 with a broken oil pipe while the battle between Clark and Brabham for the lead continued with Clark's breathtaking skill making up for his car's lack of power. On lap 65 Clark lapped Hill, Hill lapped Stewart, and Stewart lapped Bandini! Clark held on to his lead until he was forced to stop for water as his water pump was leaking. He re entered the race in 2nd place but was overtaken by Hill on lap 83. **So it was Brabham's race at 100.107 mph** from Hill's B.R.M, Clark's Lotus-Climax and Stewart's B.R.M. The fastest lap of the race was recorded by Hulme at 103.526 mph.

German Grand Prix: August 7

There were nineteen Formula 1 cars entered for the German Grand Prix and eleven Formula 2 cars in the form of Matra-Fords Lotus-Fords and Brabham-Fords. B.R.M. was still using its V8 cars as there were continuing problems with the gearboxes of the P83s. Hill chose Goodyear tyres for the race, Stewart chose Dunlop and Clark opted for Firestone. Tyres were to be of crucial importance on the damp to wet circuit. Jim Clark was fastest in practice in his Lotus-Climax, John Surtees 2nd in a Cooper-Maserati, Jackie Stewart 3rd in a B.R.M. and Ludovico Scarfiotti 4th in a 2.4 litre V6 Ferrari. Once again the mix suggested a fascinating race. The fastest of the Formula 2 cars was the Matra-Ford of Jacky Ickx which was 16th fastest overall.

John Surtees took an early lead from Jack Brabham (Brabham-Repco), Lorenzo Bandini (V12 Ferrari) and Jochen Rindt (Cooper-Maserati.) Then on lap 1 John Taylor's Brabham-B.R.M. spun off and caught fire after being shunted. Tragically Taylor did not survive his burns. At the front Brabham overtook Surtees who was then followed by Rindt, Clark and Gurney (Eagle-2.7 litre Climax), Stewart (B.R.M.), Bandini (Ferrari), Mike Parkes (V12 Ferrari), Graham Hill (B.R.M.) and Denny Hulme (Brabham-Repco). Bandini and Clark dropped back, unhappy with their tyres, and both were overtaken by Hill's B.R.M. None of the Ferraris was really in the running. **Brabham (Brabham-Repco) won at 86.747 mph** from Surtees (Cooper-Maserati), Rindt (Cooper-Maserati), Hill (B.R.M.), Stewart (B.R.M.) and Bandini (Ferrari). The fastest lap of the race was made by Surtees at 96.454 mph.

Italian Grand Prix: September 4

Two new cars made their debut at Monza, the first being the 3 litre V12 Honda which was powerful but also large and heavy, and the second an Eagle with a V12 Weslake engine. Not to be outdone, the three V12 Ferraris had more powerful engines with new cylinder heads and 36 valves. B.R.M. put its faith in the P83s with their H16 engines now extensively modified, and it was fervently hoped that they would prove to be more reliable. Problems during practice indicated that such hopes were ill founded. In the end only one H16 B.R.M. made it to the starting grid, to be driven by Graham Hill back in 11th place. Jackie Stewart was marginally better with a V8 engined car in 9th place. Lotus had a Lotus 43 with an H16 B.R.M. engine for Jim Clark, a car with a 2 litre V8 B.R.M. engine for Arundell and a third car with a 2 litre V8 Coventry-Climax engine for a young Italian driver known as "Geki". The Ferraris of Mike Parkes, Ludovico Scarfiotti, and Lorenzo Bandini were 1st, 2nd and 5th in practice. Jim Clark's Lotus-B.R.M. was 3rd and John Surtees' Cooper-Maserati 4th. The new Honda was 7th in the hands of Richie Ginther and Dan Gurney's Eagle-Weslake, less promisingly, was on the back row in 19th place.

Scarfiotti and Parkes led at the start and they were joined by Bandini before the end of the first lap. Bandini then took the lead as Scarfiotti dropped back several places. Also on the first lap Hill's H16 engine exploded. Clark was at the back of the field after a poor start but began to carve his way through it. Bandini lost time at his pit with a leaking fuel pipe and Jackie Stewart retired on lap 6 with a similar problem. Gurney had also pitted with fuel feed problems on the new Eagle-Weslake. The situation remained fluid at the front but Jack Brabham led until an oil leak ended his race on lap 8. It was now Parkes (Ferrari) who led Denny Hulme (Brabham-Repco), John Surtees (Cooper-Maserati), Scarfiotti (Ferrari), Clark (Lotus-B.R.M.) Ginther (Honda) and Jochen Rindt (Cooper-Maserati). These were

Ludovico Scarfiotti winning the 1966 Italian Grand Prix in his 3 litre Ferrari.

all travelling at high speed, in close company, and constantly changing places. At one point Ginther had the Honda up into 2nd place but then on lap 17 one of his rear tyres threw its tread and he crashed off the circuit into the forest, fortunately without serious injury to himself. It then became a battle between Scarfiotti, Parkes, Surtees and Hulme without any of them gaining a decisive advantage until Scarfiotti managed to open up a reasonable lead. Enzo Ferrari wanted an Italian driver to win and Parkes had done his best to protect Scarfiotti from the advances of Hulme's Brabham-Repco. He was helped in this by Bandini who was exactly one lap down. **Scarfiotti won the race at 135.923 mph** from Parkes and Hulme, the two of them disputing second place right to the end. Rindt literally scraped across the finishing line with a deflating tyre and parked his car at an angle on the grass. The fastest lap was achieved by Scarfiotti at 139.203 mph who was the first Italian driver to win the Italian Grand Prix since Alberto Ascari in 1952.

United States Grand Prix: October 2

Jim Clark was to drive the Lotus 43 with an H16 B.R.M. engine and B.R.M. had three P83s with a spare H16 engine on hand. There was only one Ferrari at Watkins Glen and it was to be driven by Lorenzo Bandini. Dan Gurney had the Eagle-Weslake and Bob Bondurant was given the Eagle-2.7 litre Climax. There were two Hondas for Ritchie Ginther and Ronnie Bucknum, and Bruce McLaren had his McLaren-Ford, now with increased power. Jo Siffert drove Rob Walker's Cooper-Maserati and Mike Spence Tim Parnell's Lotus-B.R.M. Clark went very well in practice to be 2nd on the grid but B.R.M. offered Colin Chapman the spare H16 engine when oil was seen escaping from Clark's exhaust. Jack Brabham was fastest in practice with his Brabham-Repco and after Clark came Lorenzo Bandini's V12 Ferrari and John Surtees Cooper-Maserati, followed by the B.R.Ms of Graham Hill and Jackie Stewart. Richie Ginther's Honda was 8th and Dan Gurney's Eagle–Weslake was 14th. Bucknum's Honda was 18th and near the back.

It was Bandini who initially led, after coming through from the 2nd row, from Clark, Ginther from the 4th row, and Brabham. The Honda then slipped back through the field on successive laps and the two B.R.Ms of Stewart and Hill chased Brabham. Both Jack Brabham and John Surtees (Cooper-Maserati) got past Clark and then challenged Bandini for the lead, while Surtees touched Arundell (Lotus-Climax) whom he was lapping and consequently dropped out of contention. Gurney retired on lap 14 with clutch trouble. The two P83 H16 B.R.Ms retired, Hill's with a broken crown wheel and pinion on lap 53 and Stewart's with an engine failure on 54, while Brabham stayed ahead of Clark at the front. Then, on lap 56 Brabham was out of the race with engine trouble and Clark found himself to be leading the race by a minute from Jochen Rindt's Cooper-Maserati. The race produced what would prove to be the only win for the H16 B.R.M. engine, **Clark winning at 114.939 mph.** After Clark's Lotus came the Cooper-Maseratis of Rindt, Surtees and Jo Siffert, the McLaren-Ford of Bruce McLaren and the Lotus-Climax of Peter Arundell. The fastest lap of the race was achieved by Surtees at 118.846 mph.

Mexican Grand Prix: October 23

Jim Clark was again 2nd in practice in his H16 B.R.M. engined Lotus 43 but had to have another H16 B.R.M. engine fitted when the one he had raced at Watkins Glen failed. John Surtees' Cooper-Maserati was on pole, Ritchie Ginther's Honda 3rd, Jack Brabham's Brabham-Repco 4th and Jochen Rindt's Cooper-Maserati 5th. Graham Hill and Jackie Stewart were 7th and 10th in their P83 B.R.Ms. Bob Bondurant was last of all in the Eagle-Weslake which had a troubled practice in the hands of both Bondurant and Dan Gurney. Gurney elected to drive the Eagle-Climax and was 9th on the grid.

Ginther came through to lead the race on the first lap followed closely by Jochen Rind, Jack Brabham, Denny Hulme, Surtees and Clark, who was having trouble with his gears. Then Brabham moved up to the front and Ginther was relegated to 3rd place before being passed with a succession of cars. It was now Surtees' turn to come through and lead from

Brabham and Rindt who were followed by Stewart's B.R.M. Hill retired on lap 18 with engine trouble and Stewart on lap 26 with an oil leak. The Eagle-Weslake had stopped on lap 14 with engine problems. **So it was Surtees' race at 95.717 mph** from the Brabham-Repcos of Brabham and Hulme. Ginther finished 4th in the Honda and Dan Gurney 5th in the Eagle-Climax. The distinction of setting the fastest lap of the race went to Ginther at 98.327 mph.

The World Championship

Jack Brabham won his third World Championship, this time in one of his own cars, with 42 points. John Surtees was second with 28, Jochen Rindt 3rd with 22, Denny Hulme 4th with 18, Graham Hill 5th with 17, Jim Clark 6th with 16, Jackie Stewart 7th with 14, Mike Parkes and Lorenzo Bandini 8th with 12 points.

The Constructors' World Championship went to Brabham-Repco with 42 points, followed by Ferrari with 31 points, Cooper-Maserati with 30 points, B.R.M. with 22, Lotus-B.R.M. with 13, Lotus-Climax with 8, Eagle-Climax with 4, Honda with 3, McLaren-Ford with 2, Brabham-B.R.M, McLaren-Serenissima and Brabham-Climax each with 1.

Monte Carlo Rally

Sadly the 1966 Monte Carlo Rally is remembered mainly for the outrage caused by the application of revised rules by the Paris based F.I.A which appeared to favour the French entries. Only completely standard touring cars of which at least 5000 had been produced within 12 months were allowed in Group 1 and those in Group 2 were penalised 18% by a handicap system which virtually excluded them from the possibility of an outright win. The Volvo and Saab entries were scratched because the organisers had failed to homologate them in time, and the controversy led to a greatly reduced number of entries. Nevertheless, the 1275 Mini Cooper S of Timo Makinen and Paul Easter was the outright winner, Roger Clark came 2nd in his Lotus Cortina. Rauno Aaltonen was 3rd and Paddy Hopkirk 4th both in Mini Coopers. All these cars had been placed in Group 1 but after the event they were taken apart and minutely examined. After this they were all excluded on the basis that they had non dipping single filament quartz iodine bulbs in their headlamps instead

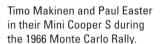

Timo Makinen and Paul Easter in their Mini Cooper S during the 1966 Monte Carlo Rally.

The Citroen DS21 of Paul Toivonen and Ensio Mikander coping with snow and ice during the Monte Carlo Rally.

of double filament dipping glass bulbs! The winners were adjudged to be Pauli Toivonen and Ensio Mikander in a Citroen DS21. Prince Rainier showed his displeasure by leaving the Rally before the Prize Giving. It must be added that the Ladies' Prize was won by the Hillman Imp of Rosemary Smith.

Targa Florio

There was a 4 litre 330P/3 Ferrari for Phil Hill and two Dino 206 cars for Parkes/Scarfiotti and Vaccarella/Bandini. Porsche arrived with one Carrera 6 equipped with 2.2 litre 8 cylinder engine, two with 6 cylinder engines in the Prototype category and two Carrara 6 models for the sports category. In addition to numerous privately entered Ferraris and Porsches there were two works MGBs, a works Prototype Sprite and a privately entered Austin Healey 3000. Then there were the Alfa Romeo GTZs and Alpine Renaults.

After brilliant sunny weather during practice rain descended on stretches of the 44 mile course, producing a number of casualties on the first lap of the race. As expected the Ferraris and Porsches thundered past the smaller cars which had started earlier, with Mitter's Carrera leading Vaccarella's Ferrari, while Makinen was still ahead of them on the road with a spirited drive in his MGB. Parkes' Ferrari had a punctured fuel tank and efforts were made to fill it sufficiently to enable it to last until the next scheduled stop. By lap six the Muller/Mairesse Porsche led overall, followed by Klass/Davis (Porsche) and Bandini/Vaccarella (Ferrari). When the Ferrari stopped for fuel the Bonnier/Mitter Porsche slotted into third place. Parkes arrived with his Ferrari severely damaged after having left the road at speed. The Ferraris of Bandini/Vaccarella, and Parkes/Scarfiotti failed to complete lap 7 and the Mairesse/Mulleri Porsche Carrera had an unchallenged lead which it held to the end. Second was Guichet/Baghetti (Ferrari Dino), third Pucci/Arena (Porsche Carrera

Willy Mairesse and Herbert
Muller winning the 1966 Targa
Florio in their Porsche Carrera
Six.

A British M.G.B. competing in the 1966 Targa Florio.

6), fourth Pinto/Todaro (Alfa Romeo GTZ), fifth Bourillot/Maglioli (Porsche Carrera 6), and sixth Lageneste/Rosinski Alpine-Renault. There were 39 finishers including Makinen/Rhodes (MGB) in 9th place, Handley/Hedges (MGB) 16th and Baker/ Aaltonen (Austin Healey Sprite) 17th.

The Baghetti/Guichet Dino Ferrari heading to second place in the Targa Florio.

The Ritchie Ginther/Pedro Rodriguez P3 Ferrari going strongly before retiring with gearbox trouble during the 1966 Le Mans 24 Hour Race.

Bruce McLaren winning at Le Mans in the Shelby Ford Mk 2.

Le Mans

There were eight works supported Mk II 7 litre Fords in the line up at Le Mans and five 4.7 litre Ford GT40s which were designed and built in England. Ranged against them were three works 4 litre 330P Ferraris, four 4.4 litre 365P/2s, three 3.3 litre GTBs and three 2 litre Dino 206s and a strong contingent from Porsche. Fastest in practice were four Fords led by the Gurney/Grant car but it was Graham Hill's silver 7 litre Ford that led at the start before the three leading Fords all pitted briefly at the end of the first lap. As the field settled down it was Gurney who led the Fords of Graham Hill and Bucknum/ Hutcherson, these being followed at a distance by the Ferraris of Pedro Rodriguez/ Ginther and Parkes/Scarfiotti. The order after nine hours was Gurney/Grant (Ford,) Miles/ Hulme (Ford.) Pedro Rodriguez/Ginther (Ferrari) and McLaren/Amon (Ford). but four Porsche Carreras were not far behind. In the course of the night all the works Ferraris dropped out, the Rodriguez/Ginther car with gearbox trouble, and the ranks of 7 litre Fords was reduced too. With hours still three Fords in the order of McLaren/Amon, Miles/

Hulme and Bucknum/Hutcherson led the race from the Porsches and this was how the race ended. Four Porsche Carreras filled the next four places, the first of which was the Davis/Siffert car. The winning car covered a record 3009.36 miles at an average speed of 130.98 mph.

Two Austin-Healey Sprites driven by Rhodes/Baker and Hopkirk/Hedges retired in the sixteenth and twenty-first hour.

The Spa 1000 Km Race

The Spa 1000 Km race was held on the same day as the Monaco Grand Prix which claimed the attention of both Surtees and Bandini. As a result of this the works Ferrari team was represented in Belgium by a single 330P3 entry, driven by Ludovico Scarfiotti and Mike Parkes. Switching from Dunlop to Firestone tyres before the race the sole works Ferrari left the opposition behind to win convincingly at 126.43 mph. The Ford GT40 of Whitmore/Gardner was 2nd, one lap down, and a second Ford GT40, driven by Scott/Revson was 3rd. Surcliffe and Redford were 4th in yet another Ford.

The Parkes/Scarfiotti 330P Ferrari winning the Spa 1000 km Race in 1966.

1967

Brabham-Repco's second year

Denny Hulme

Agreat vacuum had been left in Formula 1 in 1966 by the withdrawal of Coventry-Climax. Jack Brabham's response was the 3 litre Brabham-Repco which emerged at the end of the year as the clear winner. John Cooper managed to fill the void left by Coventry-Climax with the V12 Maserati engine, and Jim Clark had used a H16 B.R.M. engine in his Lotus 43 to win the United States Grand Prix at Watkins Glen. But it was the Ford Cosworth DVF engine that would eventually take the place of Coventry-Climax by supplying the Lotus, McLaren and Matra cars. The new Lotus 49 was not as revolutionary a design in 1967 as the Lotus 25 had been in 1962 but, keeping it as light as was humanly possible, Colin Chapman ensured that he had a car that would do justice to the new Ford engine for which it was designed. The Cosworth engine formed the rear section of the car itself, being attached to the back of the monocoque and carrying the rear suspension. The monocoque enclosed the driver's legs and extended behind his back to form the back of his seat. Chapman wanted a car which, being uncomplicated, would give his team sufficient time to concentrate on the new engine. During the year Esso announced that its sponsorship of Lotus would be discontinued and so Chapman turned to Players Tobacco for support instead. The result was the Players Gold Leaf livery which would appear in 1968. It would eventually be replaced in turn by that of the famous John Player Special. It signalled the end of an era and eventually only Ferrari would remain true to its national racing colours. Graham Hill left B.R.M. for Lotus, where he enjoyed equal status to Jim Clark, while Jackie Stewart remained at B.R.M. as the team leader with Mike Spence as his number two. The H16 B.R.M. engine formed a structural part of the P83, bearing its suspension from behind the monocoque. Reg Parnell Racing managed an additional B.R.M. team with Mike Spence, Piers Courage and Chris Irwin in close collaboration with Bourne, his drivers being available when necessary for the works team. Honda adopted a modified Lola Indy car for its heavy V12 engine which became known to British enthusiasts as the Hondola.

THE WORLD CHAMPIONSHIP SERIES

South African Grand Prix: January 2

Problems of fuel vaporisation in the high altitude of Kyalami threatened the entrants to the South African Grand Prix. Ferrari stayed away but the Brabham-Repcos were there with Jack Brabham and Denny Hulme, the Cooper-Maseratis with Jochen Rindt and Pedro Rodriguez, the H16 P83 B.R.Ms with Jackie Stewart and Mike Spence, and the Lotus 43s powered for the time being by H16 B.R.M. engines with Jim Clark and Graham Hill, A V12 Honda arrived for John Surtees, and a 2.7 litre 4 cylinder Climax engined Eagle for Dan Gurney. South African John Love had a 2.7 litre Cooper-Climax. On race

John Surtees' Honda leading Jack Brabham's Brabham-Repco and Pedro Rodriguez Cooper-Maserati during the 1997 South African Grand Prix.

day Jack Brabham and Denny Hulme sat on the front row of the starting grid and Jim Clark and Pedro Rodriguez were 3rd and 4th. John Surtees was 6th, Jackie Stewart and Mike Spence 10th and 14th and Graham Hill back in 16th place.

It was Hulme who led Brabham and Surtees at the fall of the flag but on lap 3 Brabham lost time through a spin so that the Cooper-Maseratis of Jochen Rindt and Rodriguez now followed Hulme. Stewart's engine took him only as far as lap 3 and Hill's Lotus-H16 B.R.M. crashed out of the race on lap 7, without injury to its driver. Clark retired on lap 23 with engine trouble after overheating. Out in front Hulme steadily extended his lead from Surtees who was overtaken first by Brabham and then by Rindt. Love (Lotus-Climax) and Gurney (Eagle-Climax) also began to threaten Surtees and moved up 3rd and 4th places behind the two Brabhams after the retirement of Rodriguez. Brabham lost several places when he stopped at the pits with a misfire and Gurney retired on lap 45 with broken suspension. Hulme had to surrender his lead on lap 59 to take on brake fluid and **so the Cooper-Maserati of Rodriguez won at 97.092 mph** from John Love (Cooper-Climax), John Surtees (Honda), Denny Hulme (Brabham-Repco), Bob Anderson (Brabham-Climax) and Jack Brabham (Brabham-Repco). The fastest lap of the race was achieved by Hulme at 101.876 mph.

Monaco Grand Prix: May 7

Jack Brabham's Brabham-Repco, now with a new Repco cylinder head and block, was in pole position at Monaco with Lorenzo Bandini's V12 36 valve Ferrari sharing the front row. Then came John Surtees (Honda), Denny Hulme (Brabham-Repco), Jim Clark (Lotus 33 with a 2 litre Climax engine) and Jackie Stewart (2 litre V8 B.R.M.).

Bandini went into an immediate lead while Brabham retired with engine trouble on the first lap, leaving quantities of oil around the circuit. Behind Bandini came Hulme, Stewart,

Mike Spence's H16 B.R.M. leading Chris Amon's Ferrari at Monaco.

Surtees, Gurney Eagle-Weslake) and McLaren (McLaren-V8 B.R.M.). Cement dust had been scattered on the oil from Brabham's car and this resulted in Clark taking to the escape road and consequently dropping down through the field. Dan Gurney (Eagle-Weslake) retired on lap 5 with a faulty fuel pump after snatching a brief lead and Stewart, after leading for a spell, went out on lap 15 with a broken crown wheel and pinion. The order was Hulme, Bandini, Surtees and McLaren. Then Surtees' Honda stopped with a broken piston on lap 33. Clark was making rapid progress through the field, breaking the lap record and challenging for 3rd place when his shock absorber broke on lap 43. Bandini was catching Hulme when he clipped the chicane causing his Ferrari to turn over and crash. He was instantly engulfed in flames, trapped in his car, and it took several minutes for the fire fighters, lacking protective clothing, to cope with the flames. Tragically this popular and talented Italian driver died of his burns three days later and it was a huge loss to the motor racing world. **Hulme won the race at 75.896 mph** from Hill (Lotus-B.R.M.), Chris Amon (Ferrari), McLaren (McLaren-B.R.M.), Pedro Rodriguez (Cooper-Maserati) and Mike Spence (H16 B.R.M.). The fastest lap of the race was recorded by Clark at 78.605 mph.

Dutch Grand Prix: June 4

The new V8 Ford Cosworth engines arrived at Zandvoort in two Lotus 49s for Jim Clark and Graham Hill. It would be fascinating to watch these two former rivals, who were at the peak of their careers, driving identical cars. Clark, having had little time to drive the car before the race, was only 8th while Hill achieved pole position. Dan Gurney was 2nd fastest in his Eagle-Weslake and Jack Brabham 3rd in his Brabham-Repco. Jackie Stewart and Mike Spence could only manage 11th and 12th in their recently improved H16 P83 B.R.Ms. Ferrari, sadly now without Lorenzo Bandini, had cars for Chris Amon, Mike Parkes, and Ludovico Scarfiotti in 9th, 10th, and 15th places on the grid. Bruce McLaren's McLaren-2 litre V8 B.R.M. was placed 14th and Chris Irwin in Tim Parnell's Lotus-V8 B.R.M. 13th.

Some years later Piero Ferrari wrote to me that "Mike Parkes not only was a good prototype driver but a very good engineer." He lived in Italy as the quintessential Englishman, never neglecting to take tea in the afternoon.

An official was standing right in the centre of the starting grid when the flag fell but miraculously emerged unscathed as Hill led from Brabham, Jochen Rindt (Cooper-

Maserati), Dan Gurney (Eagle-Weslake) Chris Amon) and Clark, all of them in a tight bunch. Gurney's Eagle-Weslake was the first to fall by the wayside with fuel feed problems. Hill, having commanded the race from the start, retired with engine trouble on lap 11 and Clark passed Rindt to lead the race on lap 15. Clark proceeded to power his way through the field, after quickly acquainting himself with the car while Rindt dropped back to retire on lap 41 with a broken suspension. Stewart's race ended on lap 51with brake trouble and **Clark became the clear winner** in the first race of the Ford 49-Cosworth DFV at 104.444 mph from the Brabham-Repcos of Brabham and Hulme. The Ferraris of Chris Amon, Mike Parkes, Luigi Scafiotti were 4th 5th and 6th. The Fastest lap was set by Clark at 106.487 mph.

Belgian Grand Prix: June 18

Significantly, the Lotus 49s arrived at Spa with small air deflectors on each side of their nose cowlings to create down force but they were not used for the race. Jim Clark, fresh from his victory in the first outing of the Ford Cosworth engined Lotus 49, was fastest in practice by 3 seconds. Dan Gurney was 2nd in his blue and silver Eagle-Weslake, which had been lightened by the use of titanium , and Graham Hill was 3rd in his Lotus-Ford. Behind them were Jochen Rindt's Cooper-Maserati and Chris Amon's Ferrari. Jackie Stewart was on the third row with his P83 B.R.M. Mike Spence also had a P83 while Chris Irwin drove Tim Parnell's Lotus-B.R.M.V8.

Clark seized an immediate lead while Hill was left behind with a flat battery. Following Clark at some distance were Rindt, Stewart and Mike Parkes (Ferrari). The Ferrari crashed before the end of the first lap at Blanchimont and Parkes was thrown out of the car as it turned over. The accident abruptly ended his Formula 1 motor racing career but he wasn't critically injured and the Ferrari pit held out a board to signal this news to Amon and Scarfiotti after an ambulance had brought him in. Stewart then had Chris Amon's Ferrrari behind him until Gurney moved up to third place. The battle behind them was fast and furious but Jack Brabham eventually managed to get away from Amon, Rindt and Rodriguez (Cooper-Maserati). The situation at the front then remained unchanged until Clark stopped to change his plugs on lap 12. Stewart then led by a comfortable margin, his H16 engine performing beautifully, until he began to have difficulty holding his B.R.M. in gear. In spite of being concerned about his oil pressure, **Gurney passed the ailing B.R.M. to win the race at 145.988 mph.** It would prove to be the first and only Championship win for Eagle.

Dan Gurney

Dan Gurney winning the scoring the only win of the V12 Eagle-Weslake at Spa in 1967.

Jackie Stewart bringing the
H16 B.R.M. home in second
place during the Belgian
Grand Prix.

Stewart (B.R.M.) was 2nd, Amon (Ferrari) 3rd, Rindt (Cooper-Maserati) 4th and Mike
Spence (B.R.M.) 4th. Dan Gurney also had the satisfaction of scoring the fastest lap of the
race in his Eagle-Weslake at 148.847 mph.

French Grand Prix: July 2

The French Grand Prix was held on an unloved circuit at Le Mans, not far from the
location of the famous 24 hour race. Chris Amon drove the only Ferrari and qualified in
7th place. Ahead of him were Graham Hill (Lotus-Ford) on pole, Jack Brabham (Brabham-
Repco), Dan Gurney (Eagle-Weslake), Jim Clark (Lotus-Ford), Bruce McLaren, now
driving an Eagle-Weslake, and Denny Hulme (Brabham-Repco). The B.R.Ms of Chris
Irwin, Jackie Stewart and Mike Spence were 9th, 10th and 12th, Stewart having exchanged
his H16 car for Irwin's V8.

Jack Brabham leading Dan
Gurney in the course of
winning the French Grand
Prix.

Hill led initially from Gurney, Brabham, Clark and Amon but then Clark moved up and into the lead on lap 5. Hill was in 2nd place on lap 7 . The two Lotus 49s were out in front running nose to tail and it was Hill who led from Clark on lap 11. Spence (B.R.M.) had retired with a broken drive shaft on lap 10 and Jochen Rindt (Cooper-Maserati) spun, losing places. Then Hill stopped with a broken crownwheel and pinion on lap 14 and Clark came into his pit and out of the race with a broken drive shaft on lap 23. The lead then passed to Brabham who had Gurney on his heels until the American slowed with a misfire and retired on lap 26. **So Brabham won from his team mate Hulme at 98.901 mph.** In 3rd place was Stewart's B.R.M. one lap down. Irwin had been holding down 4th place in his P83 B.R.M. until an oil leak forced him to stop just short of the chequered flag. The Fastest lap of the race was set by Hill at 102.293 mph.

British Grand Prix: July 15

The Brabham BT24s came to Silverstone with revised instrument panels which made room for larger fuel tanks in their scuttles. Jackie Stewart had a lighter and slimmer P83 which offered little improvement in performance over the earlier models. Parnell had an H16 B.R.M. for Chris Irwin and a V8 B.R.M. for Piers Courage but, after problems during practice, Courage found himself to be without a drive. It was the Lotus-Fords of Jim Clark and Graham Hill were 1st and 2nd in practice, modifications having been carried out to prevent the reoccurrence of their failures in France. The rear suspension of the Lotus 49s was also strengthened after Hill's had failed during practice. John Surtees had an improved engine in his V12 Honda. After the loss of both Lorenzo Bandini and Mike Parkes, Ferrari was once again only represented by Chris Amon. Jochen Rindt had a 36 valve Maserati engine for his Cooper, and Pedro Rodriguez was joined by Alan Rees in the works Cooper team. Silvo Moses drove the Alf Francis Cooper-A.T.S.

Starting Grid

D. Hulme	J. Brabham	G. Hill	J. Clark
Brabham-Repco	Brabham-Repco	Lotus-Ford	Lotus-Ford
1 min 26.3 secs	1 min 26.2 secs	1 min 26.0 secs	1 min 25.3 secs

J. Surtees	C. Amon	D, Gurney
Honda	Ferrari	Eagle-Weslake
1 min 27.2 secs	1 min 26.9 secs	1 min 26.4 secs

M. Spence	B. McLaren	P. Rodriguez	J. Rindt
B.R.M	Eagle-Weslake	Cooper-Maserati	Cooper-Maserati
I min 28.3 secs	1 min 28.1 secs	1 min 27.9 secs	1 min 27.4 secs

D. Hobbs	C. Irwin	J. Stewart
B.R.M	B.R.M	B.R.M
1 min 30.1 secs	1 min 29.6 secs	1 min 28.7 secs

J. Siffert	R. Anderson	P. Courage	A. Rees
Cooper-Maserati	Brabham-Climax	B.R.M	Cooper-Maserati
1 min 31.0 secs	1 min 30.7 secs	1 min 30.4 secs	1 min 30.3 secs

G. Ligier	S. Moser	J. Bonnier
Brabham-Repco	Cooper-A.T.S	Cooper-Maserati
1 min 34.8 secs	1 min 32.9 secs	1 min 32.0 secs

Jim Clark and Graham Hill leapt into the lead, followed closely by Jack Brabham. Joakim Bonnier was the first casualty, his Rob Walker Cooper-Maserati stopping with engine trouble on the first lap. Brabham passed Hill but could do nothing about Clark's Lotus-Ford up in front. In the meantime Denny Hulme was improving his position after a poor

start and overtook Brabham while Hill caught and passed Clark. Then Hill lost precious time having a collapsed rear suspension repaired by Colin Chapman, only to retire on lap 65 with a blown engine, enabling Clark to recover the lead. Chris Amon's Ferrari got past Brabham and thus they finished, **Clark winning at 117.642 mph,** followed by Hulme, Amon, Brabham and Rodriguez. The fastest lap was made by Hulme at 121.117 mph.

Jackie Stewart's 3 litre H16 B.R.M. before it stopped with transmission trouble on lap 20 of the British Grand Prix.

Results

1. J. Clark	Lotus–Ford	1 hr 59.6 secs
2. D. Hulme	Brabham–Repco	1 hr 59.38.4 secs
3. C. Amon	Ferrari	1 hr 59.42.2 secs
4. J. Brabham	Brabham–Repco	1 hr 59.47.4 secs
5. P. Rodriguez	Cooper–Maserati	1 lap
6. J. Surtees	Honda	2 laps
7. C. Irwin	B.R.M	3 laps
8. D. Hobbs	B.R.M.	
9. A. Rees	Cooper–Maserati	4 laps
10. G. Ligier	Brabham–Repco	

Retirements

J. Bonnier Cooper-Maserati lap 1 engine, J. Siffert Cooper-Maserati lap 10 engine, B. McLaren Eagle-Weslake lap 14 engine, J. Stewart B.R.M. lap 20 transmission, J. Rindt Cooper-Maserati lap 27 engine, S. Moser Cooper-A.T.S lap 29 oil pressure, D. Gurney Eagle-Weslake lap 34 clutch, M. Spence B.R.M. lap 44 engine, G. Hill Lotus-Ford lap 65 engine, R. Anderson Brabham-Climax lap 68 engine.

German Grand Prix: August 6

Formula 2 cars were again admitted to the Nurburgring for the German Grand Prix, the fastest of which during practice was Jacky Ickx's Matra-Ford at 8 mins 14.0 secs. This compared with Jim Clark's Lotus-Ford in pole position at 8 mins 04.1 sec and would have put Ickx third on the grid. Four H16 B.R.Ms were at the Nurburgring for Jackie Stewart, Mike Spence and Chris Irwin, the third being entered by Tim Parnell. Graham Hill's Lotus 49 was wrecked during practice so, only being able to complete a few laps in Clark's car, he was only 13th on the grid. The front row consisted of Clark, Denny Hulme (Brabham-

Opposite, top: Denny Hulme's Brabham-Repco which finished in second place in the British Grand Prix at Silverstone.

Opposite, bottom: John Surtees driving his V12 Honda to sixth place at Silverstone.

Jim Clark's Lotus-Ford leading Denny Hulme's Brabham-Repco and Dan Gurney's Eagle during the 1967 German Grand Prix.

Denny Hulme taking flight in his Brabham-Repco at the Nurburgring on his way to winning the 1967 German Grand Prix.

Repco), Jackie Stewart (B.R.M.), and Dan Gurney (Eagle-Weslake).

At the start it was Clark who led from Hulme and Gurney, while Hill was temporarily shunted off the course by the slower cars which crowded around him towards the back of the field. Then Clark collected a slow puncture and, not realising why his car was handling so badly, caused terminal damage to its suspension in coming into his pit to retire. Hill had to stop at his pit to have a wheel nut tightened and then, after a further 10 laps, retired with a collapsed rear suspension. The order, following Clark's retirement, was Gurney, Hulme, Brabham (Brabham-Repco) and Stewart who overtook Brabham only to stop with a broken crown wheel and pinion on lap 6. Chris Amon (Ferrari) managed to pass Ickx's Formula 2 Matra-Ford for 4th place but the leading trio were strung out ahead of him. Ickx retired on lap 12 with a broken front suspension. Gurney's Eagle-Weslake surrendered a comfortable lead on lap 13 because of a broken drive shaft, and so **Denny Hulme won the race at 101.409 mph** from Jack Brabham, Chris Amon, and John Surtees' Honda. The fastest lap of the race was achieved by Dan Gurney 103.172 mph. The Formula 2 race was won by Jack Oliver's Lotus-Ford at 96.685 mph which meant that he was the 5th to finish overall.

Canadian Grand Prix: August 27

The McLaren M5A made its debut at Mosport powered by a new 3 litre 60 degree V12 B.R.M. engine which produced 365 bhp. The car was finished in red. There was only one Ferrari, driven by Chris Amon, and one Eagle-Weslake, driven by Dan Gurney. Bruce McLaren was pleased with the performance of his new car and was 6th on the grid. Jim Clark took pole position with his Lotus-Ford and Graham Hill was alongside him. Denny Hulme (Brabham-Repco) was 3rd fastest, Chris Amon (Ferrari) 4th, Dan Gurney (Eagle-Weslake) 5th and Bruce McLaren's McLaren-V12 B.R.M. was ahead of the P83 B.R.Ms of Jackie Stewart, Mike Spence and Chris Irwin.

In wet conditions Clark pulled away from the start to establish a clear lead from Hulme, Hill and Stewart. Chris Amon spun in the heavy rain and Hulme took the lead from Clark, while Brabham and McLaren passed Stewart. Then McLaren lost places in the rain but recovered to 3rd place behind Hulme and Clark. As the track began to dry Clark closed upon Hulme and went into the lead on lap 57. He lost it moments afterwards but then recovered it again. It seemed that the Brabhams of Hulme and Brabham could do nothing about Clark until on lap 69 the Lotus-Ford suddenly lost all power and Clark's race was run. Hulme stopped at his pit for goggles, as did Gurney, and McLaren was well placed for an sensational finish in the McLaren-B.R.M. until he had to stop for a new battery. So **Jack Brabham won at 82.650 mph** from his team mate Denny Hulme. Dan Gurney (Eagle-Weslake) was 3rd, Graham Hill (Lotus-Ford) 4th, Mike Spence (B.R.M.) 5th, Chris Amon (Ferrari) 6th and Bruce McLaren (McLaren-B.R.M.) 7th. The fastest lap was made by Clark at 106.544 mph.

Italian Grand Prix: September 10

There was still only one Ferrari at Monza, driven by Chris Amon, but it was a new car with 48 valve V12 engine. Following the loss of Lorenzo Bandini, Enzo Ferrari chose not to risk another Italian in a second car and so Ludovico Scarfiotti drove the second Eagle-Weslake. A new Honda, the RA300, also made its debut in the hands of John Surtees with a new and lighter chassis and gearbox. Giancarlo Baghetti was invited to drive a third Lotus 49. Jack Brabham had a cover which enclosed the rear of his car and a Perspex wind shield which all but covered the driver, but neither was used in the race. Jim Clark was fastest in his Lotus-Ford and alongside him on the front row were Brabham (Brabham-Repco) and Bruce McLaren in the new McLaren-V12 B.R.M. Amon was 4th, Dan Gurney (Eagle-Weslake) 5th Jackie Stewart (B.R.M.) 7th , Graham Hill (Lotus-Ford) 8th and Surtees (Honda) 9th.

There was confusion at the start of the race when a man with a green flag hesitantly lowered it and Jack Brabham disappeared into the distance to be followed as quickly as possible by the rest of the field, while the official starter looked on open mouthed! Clark had made an uncertain start and Amon's revs hit the danger zone and at the end of the first lap the order was Gurney, Brabham, Hill, Clark and McLaren. Hulme gradually closed on the leaders and briefly passed both Lotus-Fords on lap 9. Clark lost time with a puncture, returning to the fray a whole lap down, while Brabham, Hulme and Hill disputed the lead. Clark set about recovering lost time and, after a quite extraordinary and unforgettable performance, came through to take the lead on lap 61. Surtees' new Honda had followed him through to second place, having taken advantage of his slip stream, but just as it seemed that the race belonged to Clark his engine cut out starved of fuel on the last lap. **John Surtees won at 140.504 mph** with Brabham's Brabham-Repco 2nd and Clark's freewheeling Lotus-Ford 3rd. After them came Jochen Rindt (Cooper-Maserati), Mike Spence (B.R.M.), Jacky Ickx (Cooper-Maserati) and Chris Amon (Ferrari). Unsurprisingly, Clark had set the fastest lap of the race at 145.337 mph.

United States Grand Prix: October 1

Cooper brought a 36 valve Maserati engine to Watkins Glen and there were two new 48 valve V12 Ferraris for Chris Amon to choose from. There was only one Eagle-Weslake for

Gurney and it had a new ZF type differential. Jo Siffert drove the Walker Cooper-Maserati and Joakim Bonnier had his own car. B.R.M. had wide wheels fitted to their three H16 cars for Jackie Stewart, Mike Spence and Chris Irwin. Jack Brabham suffered a major engine failure which fully occupied his mechanics before the race. The front row of the grid was pure Lotus-Ford in the order of Graham Hill and Jim Clark. Then came Dan Gurney's Eagle-Weslake and Chris Amon's Ferrari. The Brabham-Repcos of Brabham and Denny Hulme were next and the three works B.R.Ms were all bettered by Bruce McLaren's promising McLaren-B.R.M.

Hill and Clark shot into the lead on the first lap but Gurney overtook Clark and attempted to pass Hill on lap 2. However Clark re-passed Gurney on lap 8 and the Lotus-Fords seem to have things all their own way. Amon was progressing through the field to overtake the two Brabham-Repcos and Gurney's Eagle-Weslake before Gurney was forced to retire with a collapsed rear suspension on lap 25. Clark passed Hill who was having clutch trouble and Amon also overtook him on lap 65. Brabham, who was behind Hulme and in 5th place, stopped to change a wheel and was immediately relegated three places. Amon retired on lap 85 with a blown engine and John Surtees' Honda expired with a flat battery on lap 97. All three B.R.Ms had retired as had the McLaren-B.R.M. and only seven cars completed the race. **Clark won at 120.954 mph** after driving with great care over the last two laps while nursing a broken rear suspension. Hill (Lotus-Ford) was 2nd , Hulme (Brabham-Repco) 3rd, Jo Siffert (Cooper-Maserati) 4th, Brabham (Brabham-Repco) 5th, Joakim Bonnier (Cooper-Maserati) 6th and J. P. Beltoise (Formula 2 Matra-Ford) 7th. The fastest lap of the race was registered by Hill at 125.455 mph.

Mexican Grand Prix: October 22

B.R.M. arrived in Mexico City with their H16 engines having been rebuilt since Watkins Glen back at Bourne. Ferrari had a second car for Jonathan Williams and Moises Solana had the third Lotus 49. There was only one Cooper-Maserati and this was driven by Pedro Rodriguez. The high altitude occupied the minds of the mechanics prior to the race in Mexico City but it was Jim Clark who set the pace in his Lotus-Ford and he secured pole position with Chris Amon alongside him in his Ferrari. Then came Dan Gurney (Eagle-Weslake) 3rd Graham Hill (Lotus-Ford) 4th, the Brabham-Repcos of Jack Brabham and Denny Hulme 5th and 6th , John Surtees Honda 7th and Bruce McLaren's McLaren-B.R.M. 8th.

A confused start led to Clark's Lotus being shunted by Gurney's Eagle but he managed to get away with a dented exhaust. Clark passed Amon's Ferrari on lap 2 and Hill on lap 3 and then increased his lead in spite of having to drive without a clutch. Hill's Lotus-Ford retired on lap 18 with a broken drive shaft and Jackie Stewart's B.R.M. on lap 24 with engine trouble. Chris Irwin's B.R.M. withdrew on lap 45 lacking oil pressure and McLaren's McLaren-B.R.M. gave up on lap 45 with a similar problem. Hulme was driving a sensible race knowing that it wasn't necessary for him to win in order to become the new World Champion. **The race was won by Clark at a speed of 101.420 mph** from the Brabham-Repcos of Brabham and Hulme. The fastest lap of the race was also Clark's at 103.437 mph.

The World Championship

Denny Hulme won the World Championship with 51 points and Jack Brabham came 2nd with 46. Jim Clark was 3rd with 41, John Surtees and Chris Amon jointly 4th with 20, Pedro Rodriguez and Graham Hill jointly 6th with 15, Dan Gurney 8th with 13, Jackie Stewart 9th with 9, and Mike Spence, John Love, Jochen Rindt and Jo Siffert equal 10th with 6 points.

The Constructors' World Championship was won by Brabham-Repco with 63 points. Lotus-Ford came 2nd with 44 points, Cooper-Maserati 3rd with 28, Honda 4th with 20,

Ferrari and B.R.M. jointly 5th with 20, Eagle-Weslake 7th with 13, Cooper-Climax and Lotus-B.R.M. jointly 8th with 6, McLaren-B.R.M. 10th with 3 and Brabham-Climax 11th with 2.

Monte Carlo Rally

Further rule changes regarding tyres were seen by some to be an attempt by the organisers to favour the works Citroens, as they gave a distinct advantage to the French cars by limiting all entrants to eight tyres. Hopkirk and Makinen both got off to a winning start but their Mini Coopers were running with four studded and four non studded tyres and this resulted in Hopkirk dropping out of contention in thick snow. Makinen had already been eliminated when he ran into a large rock. Aaltonen on the other hand, who shared a Mini Cooper with Liddon, seeing rain in Monte Carlo expected to encounter snow on the mountains, and his choice of six studded tyres undoubtedly contributed to his success. The rally was won by the 1275cc Mini Cooper S of Aaltonen and Liddon, Andersson and Davenport were 2nd in a Lancia Fulvia, and Elford and Stone 3rd in a Porsche 911S.

Rauno Aaltonen and Henry Liddon on their way to winning the 1967 Monte Carlo Rally in their Morris Mini Cooper.

Targa Florio

Porsche entered three new flat 8 2.2 litre "Grand Prix" engined 910s for Mitter/Davis, Herrmann/Siffert and Hawkins/Stommelen, and three fuel injected 6 cylinder 910s for Cella/Biscaldi, Neeroasch/Elford and Maglioli/Schutz. Ferrari had a 330 P4 for Vaccarella/Scarfiotti, a clear favourite with the spectators, and a Dino V6 for Klass/Casoni. A 2F Chaparrel with a rear wing was to be driven by Phil Hill/Sharp. Filipinetti entered a 330 P3/4 Ferrari for Muller/Guichet. Alfa Romeos produced Tipo 33s for de Adamich/Rolland, Bonnier/Beghetti, "Nanni Galli"/Giunti and "Geki"/Todaro. There was an MG hardtop for Hedges/Poole, an MGB GT for Hopkirk/Makinen and an Austin Healey Sprite for Wheeler/Davidson.

Vaccarella led for the first lap but on the second lap hit a stone wall, breaking two wheels and the suspension. Mitter crashed his 8 cylinder Porsche, ending up in a ditch and Klass crashed into a bridge. The Muller Ferrari then led but during Guichet's stint the car was overtaken by the Stommelen/Hawkins Porsche. With the number of broken cars multiplying with each lap Porsche eventually took the first three places in the order of Hawkins/Stommelen, Cella/Biscaldi, and Neerpasch/Elford. The Williams/Ventura 2 litre

Opposite: Paul Hawkins and Rolf Stommelen winning the Targa Florio and establishing a new lap record in their 8 cylinder Porsche 910.

The Adamich/Rolland Tipo 33 Alfa Romeo during the 1967 Targa Florio.

Dino was 4th and the Ford GT of Greda/Giorgi 5th. The fastest lap was recorded by Muller's Ferrari at 37 mins 09 secs, a new record.

Le Mans

It was a return of the Ford versus Ferrari battle with 7 litre Fords ranged against 4 litre Ferraris. The main Ford challenge was mounted by 4 Mark IV and 2 Mark II works cars, 2 Mark IV and 2 Mark II models entered by Shelby, and a further 2 Mark IV and 2 Mark II cars entered by Holman. The Ferraris were headed by 3 works P4s for Parkes/Scarfiotti, Klass/Sutcliffe and Amon/Vaccarella. Equipe Belge had a P4 for Mairesse/Beurlys and there were additional P3s and P4s from Maranello Concessionaires, Scuderia Filipinetti and N.A.R.T. There were two Chaparrals for Phil Hill/Spence and Johnson/Jennings with V8

The 7 litre Shelby Ford Mk IV winning the 1967 Le Mans 24 Hour Race in the hands of Dan Gurney and A. J. Foyt.

The Parkes/Scarfiotti 330P4 Ferrari which finished second at Le Mans in 1967.

7 litre Chevrolet engines. Two V8 5 litre Lola Aston Martins were driven by Irwin/de Klerk and Surtees/Hobbs. In the 2 litre class there were two Martra B.R.Ms to take on the Porsches.

Bucknum snatched an immediate lead in Shelby's Mk II Ford while Surtees' Lola–Aston Martin retired after 3 laps. At the end of two hours the Gurney/Foyt works Mk IV Ford led the Hill/Spence Chaparral and behind them came two Fords and three P4 Ferraris. By 9 0 p.m the Gurney/Foyt Ford was leading two other Fords and the Hill/Spence Chaparrel was 4th. The Gurney/Foyt car held its lead in the hours that followed, in spite of frequent stops for fuel. The Parkes/Scarfiotti Ferrari was in 2nd place as it approached midnight but in the early hours of the morning Fords occupied the first three places. Then a multiple crash of Fords left Gurney/Foyt still in the lead but from the Parkes/Scarfiotti Ferrari. The result was a second impressive win by Ford, the Gurney/Foyt car covering a record 3251.572 miles at an average speed of 135.48 mph. Parkes/Scarfiotti (Ferrari) came 2nd, Mairesse/Beurlys (Ferrari) 3rd, McLaren/Donohue (Ford) 4th and these were followed by four Porsches.

1968
Jim Clark's mantle passes to Graham Hill

In 1997 the Ford-Cosworth DVF engined Lotus 49s had been fast and only required greater reliability in 1998 to make them more than a match for the Brabham–Repcos. At the same time Brabham challenged Cosworth with a new 90 degree V8 Repco engine with 32 valves and 375 bhp.

Sadly 1998 was marred by the tragic death of Jim Clark in a Formula 2 race at Hockenheim on April 7th. It was not important that Clark should win this comparatively minor race and he was unhappy with his car's performance, but there was only one way he knew how to race and his car suddenly veered off the course and into the trees at high speed, causing his instant death. T h e Lotus was scarcely recognisable and no driver could have survived the impact. It was unthinkable that the crash could have been caused by driver error and most believed that it must have been the result of a tyre rapidly deflating. Another theory was that the engine's mechanical metering unit had seized, but no one will ever know for certain why it happened. It was an immense loss to Jim Clark's friend Jackie Stewart, Colin Chapman, and every motor racing enthusiast. As well as being a uniquely talented racing driver he was a great sportsman and universally popular. Many, like me, must have been led to question whether they could or should sustain any enthusiasm for such a dreadfully cruel sport as this.

Clark had won the first race of the Season in South Africa with ease and then, in his absence, it fell to Graham Hill to lead the team to further victories in the Lotus 49B. His car was finished in Players Gold Leaf colours and had wings at the front and a wedge shaped tail. Wings to produce greater down force became an important consideration for all the teams and lessons were learned regarding the need to firmly attach them to the structure of the cars. In 1968 the Cosworth DVF engine was also used by McLaren and in Ken Tyrrell's Matras. The McLaren M7A was similar in many respects to the Lotus 49. A Matra MS9 appeared in South Africa but it was replaced at Monaco by the MS10 with a tubular subframe for the engine and gearbox attached to a monocoque. Matra was developing its own V12 60 degree 4 valves per cylinder engine for its works Matra MS11. Cooper adopted a V12 B.R.M. engine in place of the Maserati engine which had served them well in 1967, and constructed a full length monocoque to receive it. B.R.M. produced the new P126 which was designed by Len Terry and which was also powered by a V12 B.R.M. engine. It was superseded by the P133 later in 1968 with a monocoque that went the whole length of the car. The P138 which appeared later still had its own B.R.M. gearbox. Piers Courage continued to drive a B.R.M. for Tim Parnell but without Chris Irwin who had been injured in a sports car race. The new RA301 V12 Honda, had a full length monocoque and was the result of the collaboration of Eric Broadly and Toshiro Nakamura. The entirely new Honda RA302 was

Jo Siffert.

equipped with a V8 air cooled engine with a twin overhead camshaft. Jochen Rindt joined Braham and Pedro Rodriguez B.R.M. Jackie Stewart left B.R.M. to drive a Matra MS10 -Cosworth Ford for Ken Tyrrell for whom he had driven with spectacular success in Formula 3 and Formula 2. Pedro Rodriguez replaced Stewart at B.R.M. and Denny Hulme left Brabham for McLaren. Ferrari came back in 1968 with Chris Amon and Jacky Ickx, having wrung more power from its 48 valve V12 engine.

The World Championship Season

South African Grand Prix: January 1

Jackie Stewart was at Kyalami with Ken Tyrrell's new Matra-Cosworth Ford MS9, its glass fibre monocoque still unpainted. Pedro Rodriguez had the new V12 P126 B.R.M. designed by Len Terry and Mike Spence drove the slimmer and lighter H16 P83 from the previous year. Graham Hill demonstrated the 1.5 litre supercharged V16 from the 1950s. Jochen Rindt drove a Brabham-Repco, unchanged from 1967, and Denny Hulme, having moved to McLaren, drove the McLaren-B.R.M. Ferrari had three 1967 cars with increased power for Andrea de Adamich, Chris Amon and Jacky Ickx. The Cooper team, now managed again by John Cooper, had two Cooper-Maseratis for Ludovico Scarfiotti and Brian Redman. The two Lotus 49s were driven by Jim Clark and Graham Hill. Dan Gurney had a single Gurney-Weslake and John Surtees a lone Honda.

The three Cosworth-Ford engined cars formed the front line of the starting grid in the order of Clark, Hill and Stewart. Immediately behind them were the Brabham-Repcos of Rindt and Brabham while on the third row were Surtees, de Adamich and Amon. Then came Denny Hume (Brabham-Repco) and Pedro Rodriguez (B.R.M.).

Stewart made a superb start but was overtaken by Clark on lap 2 while Scarfiotti retired, badly scalded by a burst water pipe. Behind Clark and Stewart came Rindt, Surtees, Brabham, Amon and Hill, but Hill moved up steadily from a poor start to take second

Jackie Stewart in the new and unpainted Matra-Ford during the 1968 South African Grand Prix.

Jim Clark winning his last World Championship race at Kyalami in 1968.

place on lap 17. Rindt was overtaken by Brabham who challenged Stewart before dropping back with reduced power. After shadowing Hill for a number of laps Stewart's Matra-Ford retired on lap 44 with a broken connecting rod. By this time the retirements included the B.R.Ms of Spence and Rodriguez due to fuel vaporisation, and de Adamich's Ferrari after an accident. The Lotus 49s were in command of the race, Clark and Hill finishing 1st and 2nd. Rindt's Brabham-Repco was 3rd, Amon's Ferrari 4th, and Hulme's McLaren-B.R.M. 5th. **Jim Clark's winning speed was 107.426 mph and he also established the fastest lap of the race at 109.682 mph. It was a convincing performance, but sadly it was to be his last World Championship Grand Prix as he would be fatally injured at Hockenheim.**

Spanish Grand Prix: May 12

There was enormous sadness at Jarama following the death of Jim Clark in a Formula 2 Lotus at Hockenheim and also that of Mike Spence while testing a Lotus at Indianapolis.

Graham Hill's Gold Leaf Lotus leading Denny Hulme's McLaren during the Spanish Grand Prix at Jarama.

Jackie Stewart was unable to race having fractured his wrist in a Formula 2 race two weeks before. Jack Brabham was a non starter as the new 4 ohc Repco engine on his Brabham BT26 had blown up during practice. Chris Amon (V12 Ferrari) was fastest in practice with Pedro Rodriguez (V12 P133 B.R.M.) and Denny Hulme (McLaren-Cosworth Ford) alongside him on the front row. Bruce McLaren (McLaren-Ford) was 4th, Jean-Pierre Beltoise (Matra-Ford MS10) 5th and Graham Hill (his Lotus-Ford now in Gold Leaf livery) 6th.

Rodriguez established an early lead but was overtaken on lap 12 by Beltoise and on lap 13 by Chris Amon (Ferrari). The order became Beltoise (Matra-Ford), Rodriguez (B.R.M.), Amon (Ferrari), McLaren (McLaren-Ford), Hulme (McLaren-Ford) and Hill ((Lotus-Ford.) On lap 15 Beltoise came into his pit to have his oil filter tightened, smoke having been issuing from his engine for a number of laps. Amon then led from Rodriguez, Hill and Hulme but on lap 28 Rodriguez crashed into the undergrowth, fortunately without personal injury, and encouraged by his new car's performance. It was Hill's Lotus-Ford that now chased after Amon but he made little progress until the Ferrari stopped on lap 58 with a fuel pump failure. Now it was Hulme's turn to challenge for the lead but the loss of second gear forced him to settle for second place. **Hill won at 84.408 mph** from Hulme (McLaren-Ford) Brian Redman (Cooper-B.R.M.) and Lodovico Scarfiotti (Cooper-B.R.M.). The fastest lap of the race achieved by Beltoise at 86.244 mph.

Monaco Grand Prix: May 26

Following the tragic death of Lorenzo Bandini in 1967, Ferrari was an absentee at Monaco where steps had been taken to make a similar accident less likely. The McLarens and Coopers had shortened nose cowls for Monaco and the Lotus-Fords sported wings on each side of their cowls. Richard Attwood had joined Piers Courage in Parnell's B.R.M. team, replacing Chris Irwin who was still recovering from his Nurburgring crash. He was 6th fastest in practice in a P126 B.R.M, Pedro Rodriguez (P133) and Piers Courage

John Surtees' Honda passing the Hotel Mirabeau in Monaco.

(P126) being 9th and 11th, all three B.R.Ms being Len Terry designs. Graham Hill (Lotus-Ford) was in pole position while Johnny Servoz-Gavin was 2nd fastest in the Ken Tyrrell Matra-Ford. Then came Jo Siffert (Rob Walker Lotus-Ford), John Surtees (Honda) and Jochen Rindt (Brabham-Repco). Dan Gurney was at the very back of the grid with his Eagle-Weslake. Jack Oliver drove the second Lotus-Ford and was 13th in practice. Jean Pierre Beltoise had a works V12 Matra engined Matra.

Servoz-Gavin made a perfect start and opened up a useful lead over Hill, Siffert, Surtees and Jochen Rindt. Bruce McLaren (McLaren-Ford) and Oliver (Lotus-Ford) collided on the first lap and the Servoz-Gavin retired on lap 4 with a broken drive shaft. Further casualties included Jack Brabham (Brabham-Repco), Rindt (Brabham-Repco), Dan Gurney (Eagle-Weslake), Jo Siffert (Lotus-Ford) and Jean-Pierre Beltoise (Matra). Hill continued to lead with Attwood in the sole surviving B.R.M. in close attendance and they finished the race in that order with Lucien Bianchi (Cooper-B.R.M.) 3rd, Ludovico Scarfiotti (Cooper-B.R.M.) 4th, and Denny Hulme (McLaren-Ford 5th. **Hill won the race at 77.819 mph** and the fastest lap was recorded by Attwood at 79.854 mph.

Belgian Grand Prix: June 9

Jackie Stewart was back at Spa with his wrist still in plaster to drive Ken Tyrrell's Matra MS10 –Ford Cosworth and he had the Ferraris of Chris Amon and Jacky Ickx on each side of him at the front of the grid. During practice several teams had tried out aerodynamic aids at the front and the back of their cars. The Brabhams of both Jack Brabham and Jochen Rindt had the 4 cam Repco engines and there were four V12 P126 B.R.Ms for Pedro Rodriguez, Richard Attwood and Piers Courage, the last named being entered by Tim Parnell. Attwood was the fastest of them and 7th on the grid. John Surtees (Honda) was 4th, Denny Hulme (McLaren–Ford) 5th Bruce McLaren (McLaren-Ford) 6th Piers Courage (P126 B.R.M.) 7th and Pedro Rodriguez (P133 B.R.M.) 8th. Graham Hill and Jackie Oliver (Lotus-Fords) were only 14th and 15th on the 6th row of the grid. Jack Brabham, virtually missing practice through having a new engine installed, was at the very back of the grid.

The two Ferraris of Amon and Ickx led away from the start while Stewart was overtaken by John Surtees' Honda and Denny Hulme's McLaren-Ford. Ickx slowed with a misfire and, by lap 7 Hill had retired with a broken drive shaft having moved up to 10th place. Brian Redman's Cooper-B.R.M. crashed and caught fire, fortunately without serious injury to the driver. Amon retired on the following lap with a holed oil radiator, and Surtees led comfortably until his rear wishbone collapsed on lap 11. The order then became Hulme, Stewart, McLaren until Hulme's driveshaft fractured on lap 18. Stewart stopped, out of fuel, on the penultimate lap. It was then a race between McLaren and Rodriguez which was settled in favour of the McLaren-Ford, **Bruce McLaren winning at 147.139 mph** 12 seconds ahead of Rodriguez. Ickx (Ferrari) was 3rd, Stewart (Matra-Ford) 4th and Jackie Oliver (Lotus-Ford) was classified 5th. The fastest lap of the race was set by Surtees at 149.837 mph.

Dutch Grand Prix: June 23

Graham Hill was 3rd in practice with his Lotus 49B. Fastest was Chris Amon's Ferrari and, between the two of them was Jochen Rindt's Brabham-Repco. Jack Brabham's Brabham-Repco and Jackie Stewart's Matra-Ford were in the second row of the grid. Dan Gurney drove a third Brabham-Repco as he was short of engines, and was 12th in practice alongside the B.R.M. of Pedro Rodriguez.

On race day it was Rindt who led initially but at the end of the first lap he was in 3rd place with Hill leading Stewart. The latter had chosen wet weather tyres because of the uncertain conditions before the race and these assisted him in taking the lead on lap 4 and pulling away from Hill and Jean-Pierre Beltoise (V12 Matra), who had moved up in the rain from 16th position on the grid! Beltoise passed Hill on lap 50. Heavy rain was largely responsible for a crop of retirements, Hill spinning on lap 54 and Gurney on lap 56. Stewart

B G Apps

Jackie Stewart's MS10 Matra-Ford storming away ahead of the field in the rain at Zandvoort.

continued to lead, thus demonstrating his mastery in the rain and lapping all the other cars, before allowing Beltoise to unlap himself. **So Stewart's Matra-Ford won at 84.658 mph** from the Matra engined car of Beltoise with Rodriguez (B.R.M.) in 3rd place. Next came Ickx (Ferrari), Silio Moser (Brabham-Repco), Chris Amon (Ferrari), Richard Attwood (B.R.M.), Joakim Bonnier (McLaren-B.R.M.) and finally Hill (Lotus-Ford) who was classified 9th. The fastest lap was made by Beltoise at 88.561 mph.

French Grand Prix: July 7

Jo Schlesser arrived at Rouen to drive the brand new air cooled V8 Honda RA302 while John Surtees, who thought the car needed more development, drove the V12 R301. Schlesser was only 16th in practice and next to last on the starting grid. At the other end the front row consisted of Jacky Ickx (Ferrari), Jackie Stewart (Matra-Ford) and Jochen Rindt (Brabham-Repco). Then came Chris Amon (Ferrari) and Denny Hulme (McLaren-Ford.) John Surtees was 7th in the V12 Honda and the B.R.Ms of Pedro Rodriguez, Richard Attwood and Piers Courage were 9th, 12th, and 15th. Jackie Oliver (49B Lotus-Ford with a raised aerofoil) crashed in practice, and Graham Hill was beset with gear selection problems.

Rain caused some teams to put on wet weather tyres at the last minute and Jacky Ickx, on wets, was leading at the end of the first lap. He was followed by Stewart, Rindt (Brabham-Repco) and Surtees. Then a dreadful tragedy occurred which clouded the day when poor Jo Schlesser crashed on lap 3. His car turned over and caught fire and he died in the inferno. Rindt picked up a puncture from the debris while Ickx led Surtees, Rodriguez and Stewart. Rodriguez overtook Surtees after a piece of metal also from the debris was thrown up from the B.R.M's rear tyre and damaged his goggles. In torrential rain Ickx was overtaken by his two pursuers on lap 19 but he recovered his lead soon

Jacky Ickx winning the 1968 French Grand Prix in his V12 Ferrari while being followed by John Surtees' Honda.

afterwards and held it to the end. Surtees stopped to replace his goggles but resumed in 3rd place. Then Surtees inherited 2nd place when Rodriguez dropped out of contention with a puncture and gearbox troubles. **So Ickx (Ferrari) won at 100.452 mph** from Surtees (Honda) Stewart (Matra-Ford) Vic Elford (Cooper-B.R.M.) and Denny Hulme (McLaren-Ford.) Rodriguez established the fastest lap of the race at 111.285 mph.

British Grand Prix: July 20

The Lotus-Fords looked favourites to win the British Grand Prix at Brand Hatch with Graham Hill and Jackie Oliver securing the first two places on the grid. Chris Amon's Ferrari was 3rd and then a brand new 49B Lotus-Ford which Rob Walker had bought with the support of London stock broker Jack Durlacher for Jo Siffert to drive. It had a Hewland gearbox, the latest suspension, and was in every respect identical to the works cars. Jackie Stewart was back in 7th place alongside Dan Gurney's Eagle which seemed to have lost its edge since he had parted company with Weslake.

Starting Grid

C. Amon	J. Oliver	G. Hill
Ferrari	Lotus-Ford	Lotus-Ford
1 min 29.5 secs	1 min 29.4 secs	1 min 28.9 secs

J. Rindt	J. Siffert
Brabham-Repco	Lotus-Ford
1 min 30.2 secs	1 min 29.7 secs

J. Brabham	J. Stewart	D. Gurney
Brabham-Repco	Matra-Ford	Eagle
1 min 30.2 secs	1 min 30.0 secs	1 min 30.0 secs

B. McLaren	J. Surtees
McLaren-Ford	Honda
1 min 30.4 secs	1 min 30.3 secs

P. Rodriguez	J. Ickx	D. Hulme
B.R.M	Ferrari	McLaren-Ford
1 min 31.6 secs	1 min 31.0 secs	1 min 30.4 secs

R. Attwood	J.P. Beltoise
B.R.M	Matra
1 min 31.7 secs	1 min 31.6 secs

R. Widdows	V. Elford	P. Courage
Cooper-B.R.M	Cooper-B.R.M	B.R.M
1 min 34.0 secs	1 min 33.0 secs	1 min 32.3 secs

J. Bonnier	S. Moser
McLaren-B.R.M	Brabham-Repco
1 min 36.8 secs	1 min 35.4 secs

It began to rain just before the start at which the three Lotus 49Bs led away in the order of Jackie Oliver, Graham Hill and Jo Siffert. Vic Elford and Dan Gurney were left on the line with dead engines. Those who had made a last minute decision to change to wet tyres would be at a disadvantage and the three leaders were followed by Chris Amon, Jackie Stewart and John Surtees. Hill passed Oliver to lead on lap 4 and eventually Surtees overtook Stewart but the order remained mainly unchanged until Hill's drive shaft and rear suspension broke on lap 27 putting him out of the race. So the running order became Oliver, Siffert and Amon with Oliver drawing away by more than 10 seconds from his pursuers. Surtees lost the rear wing of his Honda and dropped back while Oliver stopped on lap 44 with a transmission failure. This meant that Siffert now led, pursued at close quarter's by Amon's Ferrari. The matter was decided when Amon's tyres became badly

Jo Siffert winning the 1968 British Grand Prix for Rob Walker in his Lotus 49.

worn, causing him to lose grip, and so **Jo Siffert won at 104.831 mph in the dark blue Lotus 49B of the amazing privateer Rob Walker.** It was the last major success in Formula 1 by a privateer. Amon was 2nd 4.4 seconds behind and Ickx 3rd a whole lap in arrears. The fastest lap was also Siffert's at 106.354 mph.

Results

1. J. Siffert	Lotus-Ford	2 hr 01 min 20.3 secs
2. C. Amon	Ferrari	2 hr 01 min 24.7 secs
3. J. Ickx	Ferrari	1 lap
4. D. Hulme	McLaren-Ford	
5. J. Surtees	Honda	2 laps
6. J. Stewart	Matra-Ford	
7. B. McLaren	McLaren-Ford	3 laps
8. P. Courage	B.R.M	8 laps
S. Moser	Brabham-Repco	8 laps behind.

Retirements

J. Brabham (Brabham-Repco) lap 1 engine, J. Bonnier (McLaren-B.R.M.) lap7 engine, D. Gurney (Eagle) lap 9 fuel pump, R. Attwood (B.R.M.) lap 11 radiator, J. P. Beltoise (Matra) lap 12 engine, G. Hill (Lotus-Ford) lap 27 transmission, V. Elford (Cooper-B.R.M.) lap 27 engine, R. Widdows (Cooper-B.R.M.) lap 35 ignition, J. Oliver (Lotus-Ford) lap 44 transmission, P. Rodriguez (B.R.M.) lap 53 engine, J. Rindt (Brabham-Repco) lap 56 fuel leak.

German Grand Prix: August 4

Heavy rain accompanied by fog dominated both practice and the race at the Nurburgring, creating truly dreadful conditions. Graham Hill had a revised Lotus-Ford, designated 49B2 which arrived late on a trailer. Jackie Oliver's car was hastily repaired after crashing right at the end of practice. Jacky Ickx won pole position in his Ferrari 9 secs faster than his team mate Chris Amon. In 3rd place was Jochen Rindt's Brabham-Repco and Graham Hill came next in his new Lotus-Ford. Jackie Stewart was 6th in his Matra-Ford and John Surtees 7th in the V12 Honda. Concerned about the weather, the organisers changed the grid formation so that the cars were more thinly spaced and also delayed the start in the

Jackie Stewart's Matra-Ford excelling in the rain again to win the German Grand Prix.

vain hope that the weather might improve.

When the race did get underway it was Hill who shot into the lead from the second row followed by Amon, Rindt, Stewart and Surtees. Then Stewart overtook the three in front of him to lead the race by a rapidly increasing margin, 30 seconds ahead by lap 3 and a whole minute by lap 41. Behind him came Hill, Amon, Jochen Rindt (Brabham-Repco), Dan Gurney Eagle), Jacky Ickx Ferrari) and John Surtees (Honda). Vic Elford (Cooper-B.R.M.), Jean-Pierre Beltoise (V12 Matra) and Amon (Ferrari) all became casualties of the treacherously wet road. Dan Gurney was delayed after a puncture and Ickx spun twice, stopping for a new visor without losing his track position. Hill, out on his own in a lonely 2rd place, spun and stalled. He pushed his car to roll down the slope and jumped in to re start, all without losing his place! **Stewart won after a breathtaking performance at 85.713 mph** from Hill who was over 4 minutes behind. Then came Rindt, Ickx, Jack Brabham (Brabham-Repco) and Pedro Rodriguez (B.R.M.). Unsurprisingly, the fastest lap was made by Stewart at 88.681 mph.

Italian Grand Prix: September 8

Two members of the United States Auto Club were at Monza, Mario Andretti to drive the third works Lotus-Ford and Bobby Unser a B.R.M. in place of Richard Attwood. John Surtees had a new air cooled V8 Honda and a V12 car to choose from while newcomer David Hobbs had a second V12 Honda. The Coopers and Ferraris had electrically operated movable aerofoils. Derek Bell joined Chris Amon and Jacky Ickx in the Ferrari team. Pedro Rodriguez had a new P138 B.R.M. with a 5 speed B.R.M. gearbox and a monocoque which had been extended to carry the rear suspension.

On the front row of the grid were John Surtees (V12 Honda), Bruce McLaren (McLaren-Ford) and Chris Amon (Ferrari). Jacky Ickx (Ferrari) was 4th so there was plenty for the home crowd to cheer about. Graham Hill (Lotus-Ford) was 5th, Jackie Stewart (Matra-Ford) 6th and Denny Hulme (McLaren-Ford) 7th.

Surtees led from McLaren and Amon initially but by the end of the first lap it was McLaren who was in front. For a number of laps the two exchanged the lead more than once until, on lap 9, Surtees crashed in avoiding a spinning Amon, the two being unhurt but no longer able to continue. McLaren then led Stewart, Siffert, Hill and Hulme. On lap 11 a wheel came off Hill's Lotus-Ford so he too was out of the race and on lap 34 Jochen Rindt stopped with a blown engine. McLaren retired soon afterwards his engine devoid of oil. It became a race between Hulme, Stewart and Siffert with Ickx following at a respectful distance. The race was far from over and Stewart retired on lap 43 with a blown engine and Siffert in lap 59 with a collapsed rear suspension. After this Johnny Servoz-Gavin (Matra-Ford) got past Ickx whose fuel pump had become problematic. **Hulme won at 145.414 mph** from Servoz-Gavin, Ickx, Piers Courage (B.R.M.). Beltoise (V12 Matra) and Joakim Bonnier (McLaren-B.R.M.). The fastest lap was Oliver's at 148.698 mph.

Canadian Grand Prix: September 22

Armco barriers and other safety measures had been introduced at Mosport since the previous year. Jochen Rindt was fastest in practice with his Brabham-Repco and he had Chris Amon's Ferrari and Jo Siffert's Lotus-Ford with him on the front row of the grid. Dan Gurney, again driving a McLaren-Ford instead of his Eagle, was 4th, John Surtees (Honda) 7th, Jackie Stewart (Matra-Ford) 11th and Pedro Rodriguez (B.R.M.) 12th. Henri Pescarola was on the back row making his debut in a V12 Matra. The Cooper-B.R.Ms were driven by Vic Elford and Lucien Bianchi and they were 16th and 18th.

Amon led at the fall of the flag from Siffert, Rindt and Gurney, the first two running nose to tail. Hill overtook Gurney and Surtees became an early retirement with gearbox trouble. Amon and Siffert continued to dominate the race until Siffert had to retire on lap 30 with an oil leak. Amon's Ferrari now led Rindt, Graham Hill, Gurney and Denny Hulme (McLaren-Ford) but then Hill had to pit in order to have the source of a vibration located.

Amon retired on lap 73 with transmission trouble, leaving Hulme to lead the race followed now by McLaren, Rodriguez and Hill. **Hulme won at an average speed of 97.223 mph** from McLaren, Rodriguez, Hill, Elford (Cooper-B.R.M.) and Stewart (Matra-Ford). They were the only finishers .Siffert had established the fastest lap of the race at 100.315 mph.

United States Grand Prix: October 6

Indy driver Mario Andretti drove a works Lotus-Ford into pole position at Watkins Glen and he had Jackie Stewart's Matra-Ford with him on the front row of the grid. Behind them were Graham Hill (Lotus-Ford) and Chris Amon (Ferrari). Boby Unser was back in 19th place, his works B.R.M. having a specially widened cockpit to accommodate his frame. He had experienced an eventful practice, having crashed into the Armco and he also had an engine blow.

Andretti led at the start from Stewart and Hill, with Amon falling back with a loose steering column. Then the American had to stop on lap 14 with a damaged front and it was Stewart who led from Hill, Gurney (McLaren-Ford) and Surtees (Honda). Further retirements left only six cars in the race. A slow puncture forced Gurney to give way to Surtees in the final stages and although the leading Matra-Ford had been emitting smoke for a number of laps **Stewart won at 124.889 mph** from Hill, Surtees, Gurney, Siffert and McLaren. The fastest lap was set by Stewart at 126.955 mph.

The Mexican Grand Prix: November 3

Jackie Stewart, Graham Hill and Denny Hulme all remained contenders for the World Championship for the last race of the Season at Mexico City. It was Jo Siffert who was fastest in practice in his Rob Walker Lotus-Ford and Chris Amon who was 2nd fastest in his Ferrari. Hill (Lotus-Ford) was 3rd, Hulme (McLaren-Ford) 4th and Stewart (Matra-Ford) 7th. Stewart recorded the 4th fastest time with a spare car while his race car's broken suspension was being repaired but this could not be used to determine his grid position.

At the start of the race Hill came through from the second row to lead the race from Surtees (Honda) Stewart, and Amon. On lap 5 Stewart snatched the lead from Hill and Hulme overtook Amon so the race was on for the three World Championship contenders. However on lap 11 Hulme crashed out with a failed rear suspension, and soon afterwards Amon and Surtees joined the list of retirements. Hill overtook Stewart to lead once again but Siffert intended to spoil their party by overtaking first one and then the other before

Graham Hill (Lotus-Ford) winning the Mexican Grand Prix while being followed by Jackie Stewart (Matra-Ford).

coming into his pit with a broken throttle cable. Stewart continued to hold on to Hill until on lap 38 all sorts of problems relating to a cracked chassis and a misfire affected the power and handling of his car, causing him to drop back. **So the race, and the World Championship went to Hill, at 103.802 mph.** Bruce McLaren (McLaren-Ford) was 2nd , Jackie Oliver (Lotus-Ford) 3rd, Pedro Rodriguez (B.R.M.) 4th, Joakim Bonnier (Honda) 5th.and Jo Siffert 7th. The fastest lap of the race was Siffert's at 107.307 mph.

The World Championship

Graham Hill won the World Championship with 48 points, Jackie Stewart was 2nd with 36, Denny Hulme 3rd with 33, Jacky Ickx 4th with 27, Bruce McLaren 5th with 22, Pedro Rodriguez 6th with 18, Jo Siffert and John Surtees jointly 7th with 12.

The Constructors' World Championship was won by Lotus-Ford with 62 points, McLaren-Ford was 2nd with 49. Matra-Ford 3rd with 45, Ferrari 4th with 32, B.R.M. 5th with 28, Honda and Cooper-B.R.M. jointly 6th with 14, Brabham-Repco 8th with 10, Matra 9th with 8 and McLaren-B.R.M. 10th with 3.

The Porsche of Vic Elford and David Stone winning the 1968 Monte Carlo Rally.

Monte Carlo Rally

In contrast to 1967 there was little snow to trouble or excite the competitors in the 1968 Monte Carlo Rally and it gave an advantage to the more powerful cars. This being the case it was not surprising that Porsche 911s took the first two places but, for all that, Vic Elford thoroughly deserved his win. Renault Alpines led in the early stages but Jean-Francois Piot was forced to retire with a broken distributor. Vic Elford was partnered by David Stone in his winning car. Pauli Toivonen and Martti Turkkanen came second in their Porsche 911 and Rauno Aaltonen and Henry Liddon finished third in the leading Mini Cooper S. Minis came third, fourth and fifth but the Manufacturers' Team Prize went to the Lancias of Soderstrom, Moss-Carlsson and Trautmann. The Coupe de Dames went to Pat Moss-Carlsson and Liz Nystrom in their Lancia.

Targa Florio

Alfa Romeo came to Sicily determined to win the 52nd Targa Florio and brought a 2.5 litre V8 "33" for Vaccarella. Opposing him was Scarfiotti in a 2.2 litre 8 cylinder Porsche. There was a plethora of Zagato Lancia Fulvia coupes. Hopkirk had a works MGB GT, Warwick an Austin Healey 3000 and Wheeler an Austin Healey Sprite Special. There was also a Mini Cooper Special which had an additional engine at the rear. There were two Alfa Romeo "33"s for Pilette/Slotemaker and Trosch/Gosselin.

Elford's works Porsche was delayed soon after the start when a wheel came loose and it was Scarfiotti's Porsche that made the most rapid progress with Vaccarella's Alfa not far behind it. Scarfiotti stopped to hand over to Mitter and Vaccarella was replaced by Schutz who slid into a wall wrecking his car. Mitter, having led the race, lost time having his drive shaft replaced, and so was passed by the Galli/Giunti Alfa Romeo. The Porsche recovered its lead on lap five and was then followed by the two Alfa Romeos of Galli/Giunti and Casoni/Bianchi. The Scarfiotti/Mitter Porsche had to surrender its lead again when it

The Baghetti/Biscaldi Alfa Romeo during the 1969 Targa Florio.

The Porsche 907 of Vic Elford and Umberto Maglioli winning the Targa Florio.

stopped to free the front brakes and to replace the tail pipe, so the two Alfa Romeos were back in front. After rejoining the race the Porsche finally stopped with overheating caused by the damaged tail pipe. The main German contender now became the Porsche of Elford/Maglioli and it fell to Elford to drive it over the last three laps of the race, which he did to good effect passing the two Alfas on lap nine. So the honours went to Porsche after all with the 2 litre V8 "33" Alfa Romeos of Galli/Giunti and Casoni/Bianchi second and third. The 2.2 litre 8 cylinder Porsche of Herrmann/Neerpasch finished fourth and the "33" Alfas of Pilette/Slotemaker and Baghetti/Biscaldi were fifth and sixth. The fastest lap of the race was achieved by Vic Elford.

Le Mans

In 1968 the 24 Hours Race took place late in the year on the 28/29th of September. There were no works Ferraris and it was a dual between Ford and Porsche. There were five Ford GT40s, three 4.9 litre cars to be driven by Pedro Rodriguez/Bianchi, Hobbs/Hawkins and Oliver/Muir. Porsche had four 2.9 litre cars for Siffert/Herrmann, Mitter/Elford, Strommelen/Neerpasch and Patrick/Buzzettia. There were also two 7 litre GT Chevrolet Corvettes, two 4.9 litre Mk 3 GT Lola Chevrolets, a number of 1.9 litre T33 Alfa Romeos and a 2.9 litre Matra with a V12 Grand Prix engine driven by Servoz-Gavin/Pescarolo.

All four Porsches led at first but then it was the Rodriguez/Bianchi Ford that could not be denied and held it on to the lead for the rest of the twenty-four hours, winning at an average speed of 115.29 mph. The other Fords fell by the wayside and the Servoz-Gavin/Pescarolo Matra lay second until damage caused by a puncture put it out of contention. Clutch failures reduced the ranks of the Porsches but the Steinermann/Spoerry car came 2nd and the Stommelen/Neerpasch car 3rd. Then came three Tipo 33 1.9 litre Alfa

The 5 litre Ford of Pedro Rodriguez and Lucien Bianchi winning the 1968 Le Mans 24 Hour race.

Romeos and the Piper/Attwood green 275 LM 3.2 litre Ferrari. A V8 Climax engine Healey driven by Hedges/Baker retired in the third hour with clutch trouble, and the Austin-Healey Sprite of Enever/Poole while finishing last was 10th in the Index of Performance.

1969

A most emphatic year for Jackie Stewart

With the exception of the French Grand Prix, every race in the Formula 1 World Championship calendar had been won in 1968 by cars powered by Ford–Cosworth engines, three of them in Jackie Stewart's Matra. Ford's main opposition had came from the Ferrari of Jacky Ickx but he would be driving a Ford engined Brabham in 1969. Ferrari would be represented by Chris Amon who appeared intermittently until being replaced by Pedro Rodriguez towards the end of the year. 1969 would prove to be a rather dismal year for B.R.M. in spite of having the services of John Surtees, Pedro Rodriguez and Jackie Oliver. The newest B.R.Ms were little changed from the previous year and it seemed that the team was awaiting the new P153 which would not appear until 1970. It was clear that at the end of the '60s teams required a Ford-Cosworth engine to have any real chance of success and Honda withdrew from racing altogether. Lotus fielded a little modified 49B to be driven by Graham Hill and Jochen Rindt. Bruce McLaren also made few changes, but Matra produced the new MS80 which was designed specifically for the Ford-Cosworth engine. Its monocoque was shaped like a coke bottle, giving it more space for fuel on each side of its driver and, like the Lotus, its engine was a stressed member, forming the rear section of the car and carrying its rear suspension. Jackie Stewart won the first race of the year in the 1969 MS10 and thereafter had a most successful year with the new MS80. At the end of 1969 Matra was taken over by Simca, a subsidiary of Chrysler who stipulated that Ken Tyrrell should use the V12 Matra engine instead of the Ford Cosworth.

Jackie Stewart.

South African Grand Prix: March 1

The dominance of Ford at the beginning of 1989 was underlined by the fact that twelve of the first thirteen cars in practice were powered by V8 Cosworth engines, Chris Amon being only 5th fastest in his solitary works Ferrari. Bruce McLaren was 8th in his McLaren-Ford. Apart from the Matras, the cars were little changed from the previous year but most had modifications to their wings, and John Surtees, now with B.R.M, had a 4 valve per cylinder engine. He started on the last row of the grid, in time honoured B.R.M. tradition, having failed to establish a time in practice. The teams were able to choose between Dunlop, Goodyear or Firestone tyres. Jack Brabham (Brabham–Ford) was on pole, Jochen Rindt (Lotus-Ford) was 2nd and Denny Hulme (Brabham-Ford) 3rd. Jackie Stewart, driving Ken Tyrrell's Matra MS10-Ford, was 4th and alongside Amon's Ferrari.

At the start Brabham seized an early advantage over Rindt who was followed by Hill (Lotus-Ford), up from the third row, Hulme, and McLaren (McLaren-Ford.) Then came

Jack Brabham being followed by Jochen Rindt and Graham Hill in the wake of the flying Jackie Stewart during the 1969 South African Grand Prix.

Jackie Stewart from his 4th position on the grid, and he scythed through to take the lead before the end of the first lap. Brabham lost several minutes on lap 6 with a wing failure and afterwards found that he went better without it! Rindt dropped out of contention with a sick engine. Then Mario Andretti (Lotus-Ford) progressed to 3rd place behind Stewart and Hill while Stewart continued to enjoy a comfortable lead. The two Lotus-Fords were running close together until the failure of Andretti's gearbox brought his race to a premature end on lap 32. The B.R.Ms of Rodriguez and Surtees retired on laps 38 and 40 without having really featured at all. **Stewart won at 110.622 mph** from Hill (Lotus-Ford), Hulme (McLaren-Ford), and Siffert (Lotus-Ford). Oliver's B.R.M. finished in 7th place. The fastest lap of the race when to Stewart's Matra-Ford at 112 mph, and its driver had started the Season as he intended to go on.

Spanish Grand Prix: May 4

Many neutrals were pleased to see the rampant horses of Chris Amon's Ferrari on the front row of the grid with the Lotus-Fords of Jochen Rindt and Graham Hill on either

Chris Amon's Tipo 312/69 Ferrari leading the Spanish Grand Prix.

side of them. Next up came Jackie Stewart in Ken Tyrrell's new Matra MS80-Ford and Jack Brabham in his own Brabham-Ford. Jean-Pierre Beltoise was back in 12th place in the second Matra-Ford, behind the B.R.Ms of John Surtees and Jackie Oliver. Pedro Rodriguez took up the rear in the third B.R.M.

Brabham was left standing at the start with a dead engine while Rindt took full advantage of the situation, pursued by Amon, Siffert (Rob Walker Lotus-Ford) Hill, and Brabham, who had recovered from a push start. Hill overtook Siffert just before Hill's Lotus shunted the Armco barriers at speed as the result of his rear wing suddenly collapsing instantly leaving him devoid of down force. Before a warning could be communicated to Colin Chapman, Rindt's Lotus arrived and crashed into the same stretch of Armco with another rear wing failure, his car turning over in the process. Both cars were wrecked but,

Bruce McLaren (McLaren M7C) who would finish in second place in the Spanish Grand Prix.

fortunately, neither driver was seriously injured. These incidents left Amon leading Siffert in the dark blue Lotus by a large margin with Stewart not far behind. Siffert's race was ended on lap 31 with a blown engine and Amon was out on lap 57 also with terminal mechanical problems. **Stewart was now a clear leader and he won by two laps** from Bruce McLaren's McLaren-Ford and Beltoise's Matra-Ford. The race was run at 92.908 mph and the fastest lap of the race went to Rindt at 96.023 mph. It was an excellent result for Ken Tyrrell but the race also demonstrated the potential fragility of rear wings.

Monaco Grand Prix: May 18

It was a case of make do and mend for Lotus after Spain and its drivers Graham Hill and Richard Attwood were 4th and 19th in practice at Monaco. Jackie Stewart's Matra-Ford was in pole position with Chris Amon's Ferrari alongside him. Jean-Pierre Beltoise in the second of Ken Tyrrell's cars was 3rd, Rob Walker's Lotus-Ford driven by Jo Siffert was 5th and John Surtees' B.R.M. 6th.

Stewart and Amon streaked ahead at the start while Jackie Oliver's B.R.M. retired on the first lap with a damaged front wishbone after touching the kerb at St. Devote. The two leaders proceeded to draw away from their pursuers, Hill, Beltoise and Jacky Ickx (Brabham-Ford). Then on lap 10 Jack Brabham (Brabham-Ford) collided with John Surtees' B.R.M. in the tunnel when the B.R.M's gearbox suddenly seized up in front of him. Both were eliminated from the race, fortunately without injury to either driver. Pedro Rodriguez in the third B.R.M. retired on lap 16 with engine trouble, never having really made an impact. Then Amon, who had led the race pulled out on lap 17 with a broken

John Surtees' B.R.M. ahead of Jacky Ickx's Brabham-Ford at Monaco.

Jackie Stewart's Matra-Ford leading Richard Attwood's Lotus-Ford during the 1969 Monaco Grand Prix.

differential and Stewart, having thus inherited a substantial lead, retired on lap 23 with a broken drive shaft. Beltoise also retired with a broken drive shaft on lap 23. Hill led from Piers Courage (Brabham-Ford) across the line at the end, Siffert having lost his 2nd place and, after these three came Richard Attwood (Lotus-Ford), and the McLaren-Fords of Bruce McLaren and Denny Hulme. **Graham Hill's winning speed was 80.179 mph** and the fastest lap of the race was claimed by Stewart at 82.669 mph.

Dutch Grand Prix: June 21

Following the Spanish Grand Prix new regulations stipulated that any aerodynamic assistance must form an integral part of the body. It was open to various interpretations so all the cars were subjected to a close examination. The first of the non Ford powered cars in practice at Zandvoort was Chris Amon's Ferrari and it was in 4th place on the starting grid. Ahead of him were Jochen Rindt's Lotus-Ford, Jackie Stewart's Matra-Ford, and Graham Hill's Lotus-Ford. Alongside Amon was Jacky Ickx (Brabham-Ford) and, whoever the enthusiasts supported, most wanted to see the red Ferrari put up a good showing. The only other cars without Ford engines were the B.R.Ms of John Surtees and Jack Oliver in 12th and 13th places. Lotus and Matra had brought examples of four wheel drive cars to Zandvoort, and B.R.M. had a P193 with a redesigned monocoque, but none of these cars was used in the race.

Hill out dragged Rindt and Stewart to lead away from the start and the two Lotus-Ford drivers raced against each other while Stewart was content to play a waiting game behind them. Rindt, having overtaken Hill, retired with a broken drive shaft on lap 17 and Stewart then also proceeded to overtake Hill. Behind these, several cars competed for third place including Siffert, Hulme, Amon and Brabham but it was Siffert who eventually established himself securely behind Stewart and Hill. Siffert then went on to overtake Hill and then Hill stopped to have his car checked at his pit, thus losing a whole lap to Stewart. **Stewart now led for the remainder of the race** and he was followed across the line by Jo Siffert (Lotus-Ford), Amon (Ferrari) Denny Hulme (McLaren-Ford), Ickx (Brabham-Ford), Jack Brabham (Brabham-Ford), Hill (Lotus-Ford), Jean-Pierre Beltoise (Matra-Ford) and Surtees (B.R.M.) and Hill. Stewart's winning average speed was 111.042 mph and the Scot also established the fastest lap of the race at 113.086 mph.

French Grand Prix: July 6

There were no B.R.Ms at Clermont-Ferrand and Tony Rudd had been dismissed due to the team's recent lack of success. He had been with B.R.M. since 1950 and was the architect of B.R.M's World Championship in 1962. So the only car in the race not powered by Cosworth-Ford was Chris Amon's V12 Ferrari. In pole position was Jackie Stewart (Matra-Ford) with Denny Hulme (McLaren-Ford) alongside him. In the second row were Jochen Rindt (Lotus-Ford) and Jacky Ickx (Brabham-Ford). The Ferrari was 6th thus being in the third row and Jack Brabham was a spectator as he had broken his ankle while testing.

It was Stewart's Matra that led and he was followed by Hulme's McLaren immediately after the start with Ickx, Rindt, Amon and Hill's Lotus in hot pursuit behind them. In the following laps Stewart established a clear lead over Amon, now in 2nd place, with Ickx and Rindt further behind. Amon began to drop back while Jean-Pierre Beltoise made up places in the second Matra-Ford. Hulme stopped for repairs to his anti roll bar and the order became Stewart, Ickx, Rindt and Beltoise until the Frenchman's Matra displaced Rindt's Lotus. Jochen Rindt abandoned the race on lap 23, feeling unwell. **Stewart won at 97.711 mph** from Beltoise, Ickx and Bruce McLaren. He also posted the fastest lap of the race at 98.623 mph. It was a 1 – 2 win for Ken Tyrrell's Matra team.

Jackie Stewart winning the French Grand Prix in his Matra-Ford.

British Grand Prix: July 19

The loyalty of the home crowd at Silverstone was evenly divided between reigning World Champion Graham Hill and Jackie Stewart, the latter having won three of the four Grands Prix already run and seeming thus to have the wind behind him. B.R.M. was back with John Surtees in the new P139, now with a wider body, and Jackie Oliver had a P133. It was good to see Pedro Rodriguez driving a second Ferrari and Derek Bell driving the four wheel drive McLaren M9A. Lotus was equipped with two four wheel drive cars for John Miles and Joakim Bonnier while Stewart had the option of a four wheel drive Matra MS84. The Scotsman chose his more conventional MS80 for the race instead, and the MS84 was driven by Jean-Pierre Beltoise. Stewart was fastest in practice but, having written his car off after hitting a piece of concrete in practice, had to settle for second place with a reserve car.

Starting Grid

D. Hulme	J. Stewart	J. Rindt
McLaren–Ford	Matra–Ford	Lotus–Ford
1 min 21.5 secs	1 min 21.2 secs	1 min 20.8 secs

C. Amon	J. Ickx
Ferrari	Brabham–Ford
1 min 21.9 secs	1 min 21.6 secs

P. Rodriguez	B. McLaren	J. Surtees
Ferrari	McLaren–Ford	B.R.M
1 min 22.6 secs	1 min 22.6 secs	1 min 22.1 secs

P. Courage	J. Siffert
Brabham–Ford	Lotus–Ford
1 min 22.9 secs	1 min 22.7 secs

J. Oliver	G. Hill	V. Elford
B.R.M	Lotus–Ford	McLaren–Ford
1 min 23.7 secs	1 min 23.6 secs	1 min 23.3 secs

D. Bell	J. Miles
McLaren–Ford	Lotus–Ford
1 min 26.1 secs	1 min 25.1 secs

J.P. Beltoise	J. Bonnier
Matra–Ford	Lotus–Ford
1 min 31.2 secs	1 min 28.2 secs

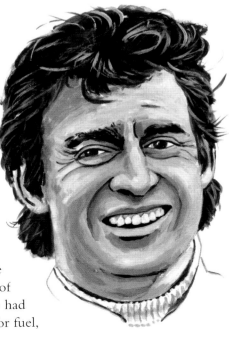

B.R.M. driver Jackie Oliver.

It was Jochen Rindt who led from the fall of the flag, closely followed by Jackie Stewart. Behind them came John Surtees' B.R.M, up from the third row, until his suspension collapsed on the second lap. Stewart passed Rindt to lead on lap 6 but, having done so, he was unable to shake the Austrian off and the two were only yards apart for most of the race. After Stewart, Rindt and Hulme came Bruce McLaren (McLaren–Ford) and Pedro Rodriguez (Ferrari). Then on lap 16 Rindt regained the lead and held on to it until lap 62 when he had to pit, as the end of his rear wing was rubbing his rear tyre. This gave Stewart a huge advantage over Rindt who nevertheless resumed the race in 2nd place ahead of Ickx and McLaren. Jo Siffert dropped back, unable to select 4th gear, and he also had to stop for fuel before the end of the race. Rindt made a further pit stop, also for fuel,

Jackie Stewart's Matra-Ford leading Jochen Rindt's Lotus-Ford in the course of winning the British Grand Prix at Silverstone.

so the race was comfortably won by Stewart at 127.252 mph. The fastest lap also went to Stewart's Matra-Ford at 129.607 mph.

Results

1. J. Stewart	Matra-Ford	1 hr. 55 min 55.6 secs
2. J. Ickx	Brabham-Ford	1 lap
3. B. McLaren	McLaren-Ford	
4. J. Rindt	Lotus-Ford	
5. P. Courage	Brabham-Ford	
6. V Elford	McLaren-Ford	2 laps
7. G. Hill	Lotus-Ford	
8. J. Siffert	Lotus-Ford	3 laps
9. J.P. Beltoise	Matra-Ford	6 laps
10. J. Miles	Lotus-Ford	9 laps

Retirements

J. Surtees (B.R.M.) lap 2 suspension, D. Bell (McLaren-Ford) lap 6 suspension, J. Bonnier (Lotus-Ford) lap 7 engine, J. Oliver (B.R.M.) lap 20 transmission, D. Hulme (Brabham-Ford) lap 46 ignition, C. Amon (Ferrari) lap 46 gearbox, P. Rodriguez (Ferrari) lap 62 engine.

German Grand Prix: August 3

Once again there were Formula 2 cars competing with the Formula 1 teams at the Nurburgring and, sadly Gerhard Mitter was killed when his works F2 B.M.W crashed in practice. Enzo Ferrari, with his eyes fixed on Monza, withdrew his entry, but the Lotus

49Bs of Graham Hill and Jochen Rindt were joined by the 4 wheel drive Lotus 63 driven by Mario Andretti. John Surtees had the latest P139 B.R.M. but, after a troubled practice, withdrew before the race, the team clearly missing Tony Rudd. Jack Brabham was still on crutches but he was able to watch Jacky Ickx make the fastest time in practice with his Brabham-Ford. The front row consisted of Ickx, Jackie Stewart (Matra-Ford) and Rindt. Jo Siffert was 4th in Rob Walker's Lotus 49 and Denny Hulme 5th in his McLaren-Ford.

Stewart took an immediate lead from Siffert, Rindt and Ickx, while Andretti crashed on the first lap and Piers Courage's Brabham-Ford ended up in a ditch on lap 4. Ickx was soon past first Rindt and then Siffert, and the crowd was treated to a thrilling race long duel between Stewart and Ickx, their two cars either nose to tail or side by side lap after lap. Behind Rindt came Hulme, Hill, Bruce McLaren and Jean-Pierre Beltoise (Matra-Ford)

Jackie Stewart taking to the air at the Nurburgring in his Matra-Ford.

Jacky Ickx, the winner of the 1969 German Grand Prix.

An airborne Jacky Ickx during the German Grand Prix.

but Ickx and Stewart were consistently extending their lead over all of them. Hill lost fourth gear and when Stewart began to have trouble selecting his gears Ickx drew away to establish a clear lead. Maintaining this position to the end of the race, **Jacky Ickx (Brabham-Ford) won at 108.428 mph** from Stewart (Matra-Ford,) McLaren (McLaren-Ford) and Hill (Lotus-Ford). Siffert and Beltoise were classified 5th and 6th but neither were running at the end. The fastest lap was established by Ickx at 110.134 mph. Henri Pescarolo won the Formula 2 Class in his Matra-Ford at 100.915 mph.

Italian Grand Prix: September 7

Pedro Rodriguez drove a lone Ferrari Tipo 312 and the new flat 12 Tipo 312B intended for Chris Amon wasn't ready. B.R.M. were also in trouble and, although it seemed certain that a Ford-Cosworth engined car would win, there was growing concern about how many engines would survive the entire race after a number of failures during practice. Jochen Rindt (Lotus-Ford) was fastest with Denny Hulme's McLaren-Ford alongside him on the front row. Behind him were Jackie Stewart (Matra-Ford) and Piers Courage (Frank Williams' Brabham-Ford). Then came Bruce McLaren (McLaren-Ford) and Jean-Pierre Beltoise (Matra-Ford). The P139 B.R.Ms of John Surtees and Jackie Oliver were 10th and 11th and the Rodriguez Ferrari 12th.

Rindt took an initial lead from Stewart who came through from the second row, clipping Hulme on the way. Then it was Stewart who led by a whisker from Rindt, Bruce McLaren (McLaren-Ford), Jo Siffert (Lotus-Ford), and Piers Courage (Brabham-Ford). John Miles (4 wheel drive Lotus 63) retired on lap 3, Jack Brabham (Brabham-Ford) went out on lap 7 with an oil leak, and John Surtees (B.R.M.) lost time at his pit for repairs, while Stewart and Rindt exchanged the lead more than once. Even Hulme, who had recovered from a poor start, had a short spell in front but then dropped right out of contention with failing brakes. It was Graham Hill's turn next to make waves at the front, overtaking Rindt to line up behind Stewart, and Courage also took his turn at leading. Beltoise (Matra-Ford) and McLaren (McLaren-Ford) were only yards away and in the last phase of the race Stewart, Rindt, McLaren and Beltoise all had spells at the front. Then on lap 64 Hill was forced to stop with a broken drive shaft, Siffert's race ended with a blown engine and Ickx was out of fuel. **So the race went to Stewart's Matra-Ford at 146.967 mph** from Rindt (Lotus-Ford), Beltoise (Matra-Ford), McLaren McLaren-Ford, Courage (Brabham-Ford), and Rodriguez (Ferrari). The fastest lap was made by Beltoise at 150.966 mph. It had been a closely fought race in which it had been impossible to guess who would cross the line finishing line first, but it was a one engine race and that was a pity.

Canadian Grand Prix: September 20

During practice Jochen Rindt tried the four wheel drive Lotus 63 at Mosport, the car having been rebuilt after being crashed by Mario Andretti at the Nurburgring, but he used the tried and tested Lotus 49B in the race. Local driver Pete Lovely also had a Lotus 49B. John Miles drove the Lotus 63 and would retire on lap 41 with gearbox trouble. Johnny Servoz-Gavin (4 wheel drive Matra-Ford) was 14th on the grid. Jacky Ickx was fastest in practice with his Brabham-Ford, Jean-Pierre Beltoise 2nd (Matra-Ford), and Rindt 3rd (Lotus-Ford). The second row of the grid consisted of Jackie Stewart (Matra-Ford) and Denny Hulme (Brabham-Ford.) Of the non Ford powered cars, Jackie Oliver's B.R.M. was 12th, the Pedro Rodriguez Ferrari 13th. John Surtees' B.R.M. 14th, Canadian Al Pease (2.7 litre Eagle-Climax) 17th and Canadian John Cordts (2.7 litre Brabham-Climax) 19th.

Stewart managed to scramble through to lead by the sixth lap after being only fourth at the start, but he couldn't establish clear air between himself and Ickx. Behind them were Rindt and Beltoise. A great dual developed between Stewart and Ickx until on lap 33 the Brabham touched the Matra as Ickx tried to find a way through. This ended Stewart's race while Ickx was able to continue unchallenged. Jack Brabham caught and passed Rindt on

Jackie Stewart's Matra-Ford being hotly pursued by the Brabham-Ford of Jacky Ickx during the Canadian Grand Prix.

lap 60 so **the result was a win for Jacky Ickx (Matra-Ford) at 111.183 mph** with Brabham (Brabham-Ford 2nd, Rindt (Lotus-Ford) 3rd, Beltoise (Matra-Ford) 4th, Bruce McLaren (McLaren-Ford) 5th, Johnny Servoz-Gavin (Matra-Ford) 6th,
The fastest lap of the race was recorded by Ickx at 113.345 mph.

United States Grand Prix: October 5

Mario Andretti drove the Lotus 63 at Watkins Glen and was 13th fastest in practice. At the front of the grid was Jochen Rindt's Lotus-Ford and Denny Hulme's McLaren-Ford. Former team mates Jackie Stewart and Graham Hill were in the second row with their Matra-Ford and Lotus-Ford. Then came Jo Siffert (Walker/Durlacher Lotus 49), Bruce McLaren (McLaren-Ford), Jean-Pierre Beltoise (Matra-Ford) and Jacky Ickx (Brabham-Ford.) The B.R.Ms of John Surtees, Jackie Oliver and George Eaton were 11th, 14th, and 19th while the V12 Ferrari of Pedro Rodriguez, entered by N.A.R.T (North American Racing Team). was 12th. Jacky Ickx spun during practice when his rear aerofoil came loose and Rindt (Lotus 49) was beset with engine problems in spite of his fast time. Bruce McLaren became a non starter when his engine blew during the warm up lap. Everyone noted that the 4 wheel drive Lotus and Matra proved to be slower than the more conventional cars.

Rindt made a good start to lead the race, followed by Stewart and Hill while Hulme was having trouble selecting his gears. Behind the first three cars came Jo Siffert (Lotus-Ford), Beltoise (Matra-Ford) and Courage (Brabham-Ford). Hill dropped to 6th place when he was overtaken by Siffert, Beltoise and Courage but then, on lap 4, Siffert retired with a broken fuel metering unit drive belt. Andretti also retired the four wheel drive Lotus on lap 4 after contact with Jack Brabham's car at the start. Beltoise dropped back with gear selection problems while, in the front Stewart overtook Rindt to gain a slender lead. Then Rindt, after hanging on to Stewart, overtook him once more when the Matra slowed and eventually retired on lap 36, the Matra having lost oil through a leaking seal. Rindt now led by a wide margin from the Brabham-Fords of Courage, Ickx and Brabham until Courage found himself to be on his own in 2nd place as Ickx retired with engine trouble and Brabham was running short of fuel. Surtees was now the nearest runner to Courage but a long way back. On lap 91 Hill's Lotus-Ford spun and overturned with a puncture and he was thrown out, having unfastened his seat belts to get his car started after a previous spin. As a result, he broke both his legs. **Rindt won the race at 126.361 mph** from Courage, Surtees, Brabham and Rodriguez. The fastest lap was Rindt's at 128.691 mph.

The Mexican Grand Prix: October 19

The Brabhams appeared to have the situation well in hand in Mexico City with Jack Brabham and Jacky Ickx on the front row of the grid. However Jackie Stewart's Matra-Ford and Denny Hulme's McLaren-Ford were little slower on the second row and all the chief suspects were lined up behind them, very much as they had been at Watkins Glen. Graham Hill was absent following his accident in Canada and Bruce McLaren's car developed a problem during the warm up, with dirt in the fuel, so that he became a non starter.

At the start Stewart came through from the second row to lead from Ickx, Brabham, Jochen Rindt and Denny Hulme. John Miles retired the Lotus 63 on lap 4 with a fuel pump failure after starting from the 11th place on the grid. Stewart and Ickx were nose to tail until a flag was held out on lap 6 following a collision between Piers Courage and Jo Siffert but, while Stewart responded by slowing down, Ickx immediately slipped past him to lead the race. Stewart dropped back to be overtaken by Hulme who went on to pass Ickx. Behind them were Brabham, Stewart and Rindt (Lotus-Ford). Rindt retired because of damage caused by running over a kerb. The order was maintained for the remainder of the race with **Hulme (McLaren-Ford) winning at 106.151 mph** from Ickx (Brabham-Ford), Brabham Brabham-Ford), Stewart (Matra-Ford), Jean-Pierre Beltoise (Matra-Ford), Jackie Oliver (B.R.M.), and Pedro Rodriguez (Ferrari). The fastest lap was made by Ickx at 108.536 mph.

The World Championship

Jackie Stewart won his first World Championship with six wins and 63 points. Jacky Ickx was second with 37, Bruce McLaren 3rd with 26, Jochen Rindt 4th with 22, Jean-Pierre Beltoise 5th with 21, Denny Hulme 6th with 20, Graham Hill 7th with 19, Piers Courage 8th with 16, Jo Siffert 8th with 15, Jack Brabham 9th with 14 and John Surtees 10th with 6.

The Constructors' World Championship was won by Matra-Ford with 66 points. Brabham-Ford was 2nd with 49, Lotus-Ford 3rd with 47 points, McLaren-Ford 4th with 38 points, B.R.M. and Ferrari perhaps appropriately equal 5th with 7 points.

Monte Carlo Rally

In 1969 there were two rallies in one, each following the same routes and each taking part in the same tests. The Monte Carlo Rally was for Groups 1 to 3 cars and the Rallye Mediterranee for Groups 4 to 6. There was little snow to contend with but the most challenging sections were one of 12 hours and another of 25 hours on the Alpine roads with special tests. The previous year's winners Elford and Stone crashed their Porsche and so were eliminated, and the Lancia Fulvia of Aaltonen and Lidden destroyed itself after coming off the road and rolling down the side of the mountain. Both occupants remained in their car and were uninjured. The outright winners were Bjorn Waldegarde and Lars Helmer in a Porsche 911S. Gerard Larrousse was 2nd in the Monte Carlo Rally and 3rd overall. The Rallye Mediterranee was won by Harry Kallstrom and Gunner Haggborn in a 1.6 litre Lancia Fulvia and they were 2nd overall. The highest place British car was the Ford Escort of Piot and Todt which was 6th in the Monte Carlo Rally and 6th overall.

Targa Florio

There were no Ferraris in the 53rd Targa Florio as Enzo Ferrari was concentrating all his efforts on the 1000 kilometre race at Monza. Porsche had six 3 litre 8 cylinder 908s, four of which were to be driven by Mitter/Schutz, Redman/Attwood, Elford/Maglioli and Herrmann/Stommelen. Spoerry/Toivonen were given a special 911. There were two V8 Nomad-B.R.Ms but the main challenge to Porsche was the 2.5 litre Alfa Romeo "33" of Vaccarella/de Adamich. Beding/Capell had an Austin-Healey Sprite and Smith/Faure a 2.5 litre Triumph TR. One of the Nomad B.R.Ms was written off during practice.

Soon after the start of the race the order amongst the big boys was Elford, Mitter,

Stommelen, Vaccarella, and Attwood. Elford held on to his lead from Mitter on to the
second lap but, to the disappointment of the partisan spectators, Vaccarella's Alfa Romeo
was under performing. On the fourth lap Elford spun and lost the lead to the Mitter/
Schutz Porsche, and Porsches held the first three places in the order of Schutz, Herrmann
and Redman, Elford having stopped to give way to Maglioli. Soon afterwards the sole
works Alfa Romeo retired with engine trouble after having been circulating in 4th place.
The only opposition to the leading Porsches was that of the privately entered 6 cylinder
2 litre "33" Alfa Romeo of Pinto/Alberti. At the finish it was Mitter/Schutz (Porsche)
who won. 2nd came the Elford/Maglioli Porsche, 3rd the Herrmann/Stommelen Porsche,
4th the von Wendi/Kauhsen Porsche and 5th the Pinto/Alberti Alfa Romeo. The lap
record was broken by Vic Elford.

Le Mans

The strongest contender in 1969 seemed to be Porsche with four 4.5 litre 12 cylinder
917 coupes. The German team also had three 908 coupes and one open 908, all with 3
litre 8 cylinder engines. Ferrari brought two 313P cars for Amon/Schetty and Rodriguez/
Piper, and Matra had four cars with V12 Grand Prix engines. There were two 5 litre Ford
GT40s in the Gulf Oil camp for Ickx/Oliver and Hobbs/Hailwood.

The 917 Porches of Stommelen and Elford led at the start but sadly John Woolf lost his
life when he crashed on the first lap and his car caught fire. Amon was eliminated from
the race when his Ferrari ran into the wreck. The leading Porsches encountered various
problems but the Elford/Redman 917 was in front most of the time while the Rodriguez/
Piper Ferrari lost time with gearbox troubles. In the early hours three Porsches led from
the two blue and orange Ford GT40s. The Ferrari finally stopped at 5 30 a.m without any
usable gears and by this time only two of the three leading Porsches remained. Five hours
later the leading 917 Porsche developed gearbox problems and had to surrender a
seemingly unassailable lead. The second Porsche was soon out of the race due to the same
cause. The Ickx/Oliver Ford now inherited the lead with yet another Porsche slowly
overhauling it. The Herrmann/Larrousse Porsche 908 led when the Ford came in to refuel
and the race came alive when the two cars battled for the lead in the remaining few hours,
with first one and then the other in front, interchanging several times on each lap. It was
the Ford that crossed the line in front the only time that it really mattered, winning at an
average speed of 129.400 mph. After the Herrmann/Larrousse Porsche 908 came the
Hobbs/Hailwood GT40 which in turn was flowed by the 3 litre Matra of Beltoise/
Courage. A Healey driven by Baker/Harris retired in the fourth hour when debris left by
the accident on the first lap punctured its radiator.

IFS AND BUTS

A B.B.C. radio commentator back in the 1960s once made the observation that "there are no ifs and buts in motor racing." In a sense he was right because, in the final analysis, all that matters is who crosses the finishing line first. There are no championship points awarded for running out of fuel on the last lap or for being shunted off the circuit on the last bend. Yet it must also be said that it is the intriguing ifs and buts of motor racing that exercise the minds of enthusiasts everywhere, and what else would they talk about on Saturday nights down at their local? In any case the incomparable Murray Walker has pointed out that FI spells IF backwards!

In the 1960s every spectator must have come away after the races with "what if" reverberating in his or her mind. My brief accounts of the events reveal how often in those days spins, crashes and mechanical failures caused constant changes on the Leader Board. What if this car's suspension hadn't collapsed? What if that car's brakes hadn't faded? The questions were endless. What if the British teams had got their way and the 2.5 litre Formula had been extended for another five years? What if Mercedes Benz had returned to Formula 1 in the 1960s? What if Coventry-Climax had been able to supply Lotus and Cooper with its 3 litre flat 16 engine in 1966?

What if Jim Clark had mercifully survived his crash at Hockenheim? All the drivers were shocked and traumatised by that devastating event, thinking that if it could happen to Clark it could happen to any of them. It seemed incredible that a driver of such consummate skill could have inexplicably left the road so suddenly and at such a high speed.

In retrospect some of the questions which might have been posed at the end of 1969 can be easily answered now. Sadly, in 1970 Jochen Rindt had his World Championship awarded posthumously. The Ford DFV continued to be dominant for many years to come, winning its last world Championship race at Detroit in 1983. In 1970 Ken Tyrrell would build the Tyrrell-Fords with which Jackie Stewart would win the World Championship in 1971 and 1973.

I cannot conclude "Jim Clark to Jackie Stewart" without a closer look at what happened to Jackie Stewart after he won his first World Championship. 1970 was a disappointing year for him as, after Matra insisted that he should use Matra engines, Ken Tyrrell chose to opt for March cars instead. Stewart won the Race of Champions and the Spanish Grand Prix that year but the March 701 proved to be no match for the Lotus 72. Necessity being the mother of invention, Ken Tyrrell built the Derek Gardner designed Tyrrell-Ford in record time. It suffered teething troubles when it appeared towards the end of 1970, but the Tyrrell-Ford 003 enabled Jackie Stewart to win the Spanish, Monaco, French, British, German and Canadian Grands Prix in 1971 thus gaining his second World Championship. Remarkably, the Tyrrell was the only Ford engined car to win that year, the other events in the calendar being won by B.R.M. and Ferrari. 1972 was a dismal year for

Jackie Stewart as he was laid low with a gastric ulcer. Nevertheless he won the French, Canadian and United States Grands Prix towards the end of the Season to finish second in the World Championship to Emerson Fittipaldi's Lotus-Ford. Fit again in 1973, Stewart won the South African, Belgian, Monaco, Dutch, German and United States Grand Prix and his third World Championship. It had been a closely guarded secret that he would retire at the end of the year, and it ended tragically at Watkins Glen when Stewart's team mate and friend Francois Cevert was killed in practice after his car struck the Armco in the Esses at high speed.

The death of Cevert, which ever after weighed heavily upon the minds of Ken and Norah Tyrrell, reminds us that motor racing in the 1960s contained lows as well as highs, moments of great triumph and moments of deep tragedy. It was the nature of the Sport. Today racing drivers sit in immensely strong tubs which are capable of surviving almost any impact while the rest of their cars may fly apart. Circuits have wide run off areas so that drivers have been known to ram each other with impunity. Spectators are placed at a considerable distance from the track where they can at least spot the cars, if not the drivers, in safety. Of course all these changes were essential for the survival of the sport itself, and they are amply justified by the lives that have been saved. Yet we cherish our memories of motor racing in the 1960s, during that era which was so different from our own today.

Jackie Stewart winning the
1971 German Grand Prix in his
Tyrrell-Ford.